THE 21ˢᵗ-CENTURY MIND

AshaPress
1400 Earlshire Place
Plano Texas 75075

KDP ISBN 9798675880522
Bowker 978-0-9909005-5-9
1 2 3 4 5 6 7 8 9 10

THE 21ST CENTURY MIND

Learn and teach a path to better thinking

BRUCE W. HASENYAGER

AshaPress
Plano Texas USA
2020

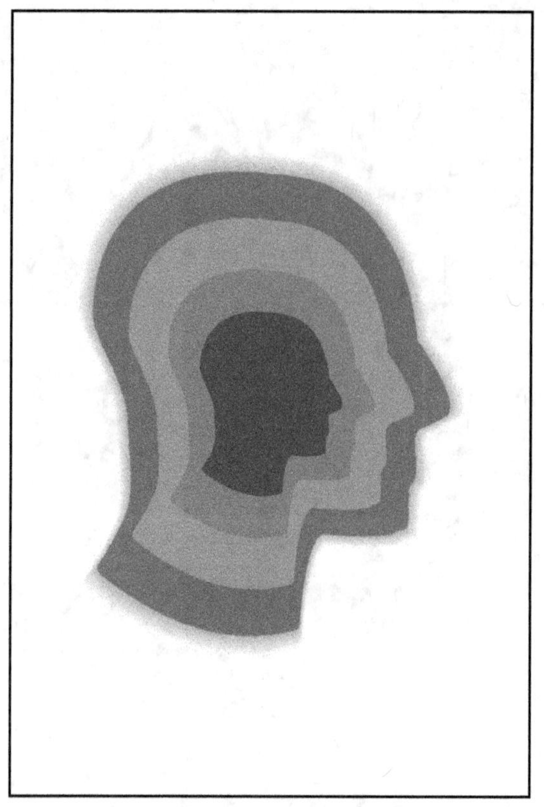

Contents

Dedicated to the young minds of the world, with hope, trust, and confidence in their superpower.

Introduction

WOULD YOU LIKE a better world? Safer, more secure, wealthier? Sure, you would. We all would. There is one thing – a relatively simple, inexpensive thing – that we can do to create this better world. We can teach our children to think better (and maybe learn to think better ourselves).

This book will convince you that there is a simple, inexpensive change we can make to our education system that will help our children learn to think better. Along the way, the book introduces a description, a mental model, of how thinking works. It's this simple model that will change education for the better.

In this book about thinking, let's be clear: we're concerned with minds, not brains.

Human beings didn't get to be Earth's most successful species because we have a brain; every creature bigger than a fly has a brain. We dominate the world because every man and woman has a mind. So, for this book, we will leave the fine details of brain plumbing, wiring, and chemistry to medical science. This book is about teaching kids about their minds and how to talk about thinking.

The need is not new. The ancients cast light on the importance of understanding the parts, functions, and limitations of the human mind. Even before the School of Athens, every examination of the nature of man has concluded that our minds distinguish us from lesser animals, and the mind is the center on which our free will pivots. The new thing here is our assertion that it isn't necessary to wait for Psychology 101 or a degree in philosophy to get a useful understanding of the parts and functions of the mind. Equipping kids for better thinking is possible, necessary, and not that hard. But we aren't doing it.

What's missing? We teach the facts and processes of reading and writing, arithmetic and mathematics, science, civics, history, and all the rich knowledge humans have accumulated. We teach all the raw materials of thinking, so, what's missing?

The missing part: we don't teach about the mind. We don't explain the role of the human superpower. We don't give our children the words and ideas necessary to talk about minds and how we use them. We don't explain the power of their minds or the limitations of that power. We work diligently to teach the kids how to think, but we never describe, explain, or even name the thinking tool. How can we possibly teach better thinking if we can't talk about the mind?

This book will persuade you that teaching children a suitable mental model of the human mind will fill a critical gap in our education system.

We will explore a straightforward model of the human mind as a foundation and framework for better thinking. Just as knowing the parts and functions of a car, a computer, or even a coffee pot will improve the way we drive, work, or brew, knowing the parts and functions of the mind will improve the way we think. A suitable mental model of mind leverages all learning – formal and informal.

When we teach children the parts and functions of their minds, they are ready to appreciate the incredible power of this most valuable tool ever created. They more readily grasp the value of learning. They begin to understand the mind's limitations and the cautions needed when using it. They identify themselves with their minds and see the quality and ability of their minds as critical components of self,

self-worth, and self-esteem. They see the connection between the quality of thinking and the quality of life.

Section One presents a straightforward model of the mind, its parts, and its functions. For convenience, we call this the 21st-Century Mind model. Read attentively, and you will unavoidably absorb the model. It's simple. You'll find it makes sense and fits with your personal experience. You may find it interesting, even exciting, to have the pieces of your mind identified and laid out for easy examination. Or you may think to yourself, "I knew that," and perhaps you did. Wouldn't it be great if everybody knew it? Wouldn't it be great if our kids knew it? They could, but sadly they don't.

In **Section Two**, we discover more about the 21st-Century Mind and use its vocabulary to discuss some things our culture has done to protect us from the limitations of our human minds and the folk wisdom we have inherited about dealing with those limitations. An appreciation for the mind's limitations is vital to good thinking.

After you've read the 21st-Century Mind model, you may ask, "Okay, now I've got it; what do I do with it?" The answer: you can use it to think about the mind, and you will undoubtedly be better prepared to talk about thinking.

- You can discuss thinking more efficiently and effectively with other people who share the model.
- You can talk to the kids more efficiently and effectively about thinking – understanding, investigation, decision-making, communicating, cooperating, or conflict-resolution.
- You can examine your thinking – Why did I do that? Why have I always done it that way? Why do I believe that? What do I really know about that?
- You can better imagine other people's thinking – How could she do that? Why does she think that? Are they evil, ignorant, or misguided?

Better thinking about thinking will stamp out a lot of bad feelings and bad decisions. Knowing how we use our minds to understand things, if we think about it, leads to less misunderstanding and fewer errors. Knowing how our minds filter reality and just how much we can trust what we "know" unavoidably leads to more prudence and less stubbornness. Knowing about the shortcuts our subconscious minds take and the biases that surround every thought leads to care and caution. Appreciating the complexity of how our minds and bodies influence each other is a path to humility. Imagining the workings and limitations of each other's minds is the path to compassion. Better thinking about thinking is a prerequisite to wisdom.

It is absolutely necessary to have a mental model of the mind to think about thinking. We need the model to name the parts and describe the functions. You can't talk about something you can't think about and vice versa. We can't teach our children better thinking unless we can talk about the tool we use to do the thinking.

Section Three presents an outline of how we can introduce the 21ˢᵗ-Century Mind into the normal progression of elementary and secondary education. The book concludes with a top-level plan of how the idea of teaching the 21ˢᵗ-Century Mind to our children can become a reality in our complex economic and political environment.

⁊ ⁊ ⁊ ⁊ ⁊ ⁊

It's fair to ask, "Why write this book? Why write it now?" There is a small answer and a big one.

The small answer is a personal one. In the last couple of decades, I've sorted through my personal thinking and benefited enormously. In twenty years, I have traded chaos, pain, and confusion for peace, comfort, and serenity. I largely credit a useful understanding of my own mind – its strengths, quirks, and limitations, and I would like to share this gift of a better life with as many people as I can. I think kids are the right place to start.

The broader answer is, I write this book now because we, all of us and all who will come after us, have entered a new era in which the human mind, our superpower, has opened the door not only to huge advancement but also to huge dangers. We are the first generation of humans who, intentionally or not, can put an end to all of us.

Up until recently, human thoughts and decisions, while they could be horribly wrong, could, at worst, only be bad for some of us. Admittedly the worst decisions could be bad for a lot of us, but no pattern of thought or decision, no matter how awful, could profoundly affect us all. Up until recently, that is.

At least 2,000 generations have been thinking and making decisions, good and bad, since humans began. Even the most consequential of these decisions affected the lives of, at most, millions of us. Now, for the first time in history, human choices can affect us all. Some of the possibilities are terrifying. The worst depredations of our past pale in contrast to our present potential to do ourselves and each other harm. Terminal harm. Never before have humans had the power to destroy humanity. Now we do. Healthy thinking and making good decisions and the right choices have become a matter of survival for us all. If you're skeptical, consider the parade of horribles in the box on the next page.

Despite these potential disasters, we will continue to affect our environment, make weapons and robots, create artificial intelligences, and control the fundamental processes of life. We won't stop, and now there are existential risks to bad decisions and unintended consequences.

Avoiding these disasters isn't a given, and there won't be any science-fiction happy ending in the real world. We humans have to think, choose, and decide better, more carefully than we have ever done before. There is no "do-over" after extinction. Today's toddlers are the ones who will avoid these terrible mistakes ... or make them. What better insurance than to give our children a better grasp of the superpower that could take us to the stars or could end us all?

Horribles

- Modern war with nuclear and biological weapons accidentally exterminates humans.
- Robots replace all human work; apathy and depression become epidemic, and suicide and failure to reproduce drop humans beneath a sustainable population.
- Artificial intelligences take control of all the devices in the world, decide that human beings are unnecessary, and eliminate us.
- The accidental release of a genetically engineered pathogen causes an incurable plague.
- Unforeseen consequences involving genetically modified food sources make us vulnerable to sudden, irreversible famine.
- Flawed design of nano-replicators causes a runaway reaction that converts everything that isn't a nano-replicator into a nano-replicator.
- And, no doubt, more to come.

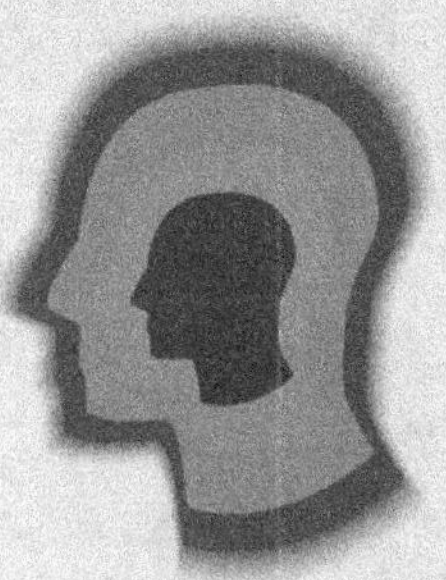

A SUITABLE MODEL OF MIND

Based on work by Albert P. Ryder
Albert Pinkham Ryder painted this mysterious image called The Temple of the Mind based on Edgar Allan Poe's poem "The Haunted Palace." In a 1907 letter, Ryder said the work pictures the finer attributes of the mind as the Three Graces who stand in the center. On the left is a ruined Temple where a fiendish figure dances gleefully, luring the child in the center away from the Graces. A warning from the past, perhaps.

Chapter 1
The Basics of a Mind

WE WANT OUR KIDS TO HAVE a suitable mental model of mind but, before we can even start, we need to be sure that the kids know what a "mind" is and what a "mental model" is. Fortunately, even very young kids can grasp these ideas with a little help.

Conversation about a mind

The dialog below is the first of several that illustrate how we might approach children with these ideas. This first one is between a tutor and a five-year-old named Bobby. Bobby is very interested in stickers of the figures he knows from his games and videos. He pastes them in his sticker book. ("T" for tutor, "S" for student.)

T. Do you know what your mind is?

S. (distracted with sticker book) No.

T. If you can tell me what your mind is, I think I can find a new sheet of stickers.

S. (interested) I like stickers.

T. Do you want to know what your mind is?

S. I guess so.

T. (slow with emphasis) Your mind is the part of you that makes you you.

S. (puzzled) Like my name?

T. That's a good guess, but your mind is something even more important than your name. Want to see how?

S. Okay.

T. What's your name?

S. (perks up) Silly! You know my name. I'm Bobby!

T. Okay, Bobby. Let's pretend that your name is Sammy instead of Bobby. Is that okay, Sammy? Just for a minute?

S. Well … okay.

T. (in a new tone) Sammy, do you remember what you had for breakfast?

S. Cheerios!

T. Sammy, do you remember how old you are?

S. Five … and a quarter!

T. Sammy, what's your favorite color?

S. Red!

T. Sammy, do you see that picture on the wall? What color is the doggie?

S. It's black and white.

T. (back to normal tone) Okay. Now you're Bobby again. You had cheerios for breakfast? You're five (and a quarter) years old? Your favorite color is red? And, you can see the black and white dog in the picture. Are all these things true?

S. (slowly) I guess.

T. So all those things are true whether I call you Sammy or Bobby, right?

S. Yeah …

T. Well, all those things — your breakfast, your age, your favorite color, and what you see on the wall – they are all you even if I call you a different name. Right?

S. I guess.

T. (slowly with emphasis) Those things — memories and things you like and things you know and things you see – are what make you

> special. They're part of what makes you just who you are. They are things in your mind no matter what your name is. Agree?
>
> S. (nodding) Okay. In my mind.
>
> T. That's why I say that your mind is the part of you that makes you you. Everybody has a mind, and all our minds are different. Got it?
>
> S. Can I have stickers now?

This conversation is about the most basic question, "what is a mind?" Mind is an abstract idea, but one a child can understand. The sense of self develops early, and by age four or five, a child understands from interactions with caregivers that he is a unique individual. With a little help, he can have a 21st-Century Mind model and understand that having a mind is an essential part of being human. Once our five-year-old gets the idea of what a mind is, other teaching opportunities arise.

- What do we use our minds for?
- What parts does a mind have?
- How does it work?
- What are the mind's limitations?

These concepts equip us, both students and teachers, to improve the quality of our thinking. In the sections below are some slightly more grown-up versions of the answers.

What is a mind?

My mind is the part of me that makes me "me. " When I say things like "my arm, my body, my brain," it is my mind that is making the claim. We know for sure that a body without a mind isn't a person, and, as far as we can be sure, a mind can't exist without a body. We understand that mind and body are different things. Philosophers call this understanding "dualism." They argue about it. As a practical matter, however, we all have personal experience that supports such a belief.

The details of how mind and body are connected are obscure. Explaining the connection is so difficult, philosophers and cognitive scientists have started calling it the "hard problem" of consciousness (Chalmers pp. 80-86). And they mean really really hard. Fortunately, in this book, we don't have to solve that problem. We will follow our intuition and understand consciousness as the feeling inside us that insists "I'm a person" and call the part of me that makes that insistent claim *my mind.*

What does a mind do?

Simply put, minds think, that's what they do. Thinking is private. I know that I am doing it, but you can't know unless I tell you. I can say that I see, hear, or smell something, but you have to take my word for it and rely on my report. I can say, for instance, "I believe in justice," but you can't know if I do believe in justice or even precisely what "justice" means to me. I can decide to do something, "drive to the grocery store," for example, but unless I really go, only I know about my decision. Of course, I could tell you, "I've decided to go to the grocery store," but unless I actually do it, my statement is only a statement, not proof. Thinking is private.

Conversation about the mind's functions.

Thinking is private, but it's not secret. We all know that we think, and we also know that other people think too. It's important to think about what our minds do, so let's look at an example of how even very young people can get involved in thinking about thinking. Here is a conversation between Sandy, a bright nine-year-old, and her tutor.

T.	Do you recognize this list?	Investigate
S.	Sure. That's the list of the things that we do with our minds. Right?	Create, invent, and innovate Evaluate Plan
T.	Yes, that's right. Do you remember what the activities involve?	Coordinate/cooperate Compete
S.	Yes. I think I do.	Conflict
T.	Can we test that so you can make sure?	Resolve conflict Communicate
S.	Okay.	

T. I'll say one of the things we use our minds for, and you give me an example. Okay.

S. Uh-huh.

T. We use our minds to investigate things. Okay, can you give an example of how we do that?

S. My Mother asked me what kind of canned soup we had, so I looked in the cupboard, wrote down the name of each type of soup, and gave her the list.

T. Very good. You investigated the soup supply. Let's try Create. Remember, create means inventing or coming up with something new.

S. Let me think. Oh, I know. My girlfriends and I made up a new jump rope song. Want to hear it?

T. Sure.

S. (chanting) Jump-rope jump-rope, don't you see/my mind's the part that makes me me/Jump-rope jump-rope, it's not funny/without my mind I'm just a dummy.

T. Wow! That's certainly an excellent example of your mind creating. And it's an example of another thing that minds do. Can you tell me what it is?

S. Let me think … oh, we cooperated to make the song. Right?

T. Yes. You and the girls coordinated your creativity. All your minds worked together.

S. Hey, you know what. I think I can make up a story of using my mind to do all the rest of the things on the list. Let me see … Evaluate, Plan, hmmm. How about this story:

Sarah and I were trying to decide what to do. I wanted to go shopping, and she wanted to watch TV. To decide which to do, we went rock-paper-scissors. We cooperated on how to decide. She always goes paper first, so I went scissors and beat her the first time. That's competing. Then Sarah said, "Okay, where shall we go to shop?" We talked about either walking downtown or going to the mall. There are more stores at the mall, but it's too far to walk. That's evaluating. Sarah and I thought about it together. That was cooperating. We said having lots of different stores was more important than how far we had to go, so we decided to go to the mall on the bus. That was planning.

T. That's wonderful! So many different kinds of thinking in one story.

Just to review, here's the list of activities that we use our minds for. We:

- **Investigate.** We intentionally gather information, organize it, and remember it.
- **Create, invent, and innovate.** We imagine things in reality that we have never perceived and events we have never experienced.
- **Evaluate.** We compare real things or imagined situations.
- **Plan.** We imagine possible alternative futures, compare different ways we could make those futures happen, and decide among the different alternatives.

In addition to thinking on our own, there are also mind activities that require us to work together and combine our thinking:

- **Coordinate/cooperate.** We communicate with each other, agree on an objective, plan a way to achieve it, and decide who does what and when.
- **Compete/conflict/resolve conflict.** We compare our efforts or our group's efforts to others. We imagine how our efforts and theirs will interact. When we recognize a conflict, we investigate it. We evaluate the cost of leaving the conflict unresolved. We plan a strategy to win the conflict or resolve it.
- **Communicate, act, and adjust.** We respond to the actions of others.

Of course, we are not always engaged in doing these "productive" activities. We ponder, we reminisce, we daydream. Sometimes we just "veg out" listening to music, appreciating something beautiful, or simply relaxing. These things, too, are thinking; minds seldom stop. Minds have tools that do these essential functions, and, when we think, we mobilize the tools in intricate patterns. We can consciously control our thoughts, use our minds productively, or we can just let them wander and "chill." Our minds are busy all the time, ceaselessly doing the basic things they have evolved to do.

Why do we think?

We all think. Thinking is a shared feature of being a human being. It's awesome, but it's a mixed blessing. Some of the things we know, we remember, or we imagine cause us discomfort or pain. If thinking hurts me, why do it? Because we have no choice. We can't stop thinking. A mind is a machine that just keeps running until the body it lives with dies.

Most animals are not as conscious as we are; they operate more on instinct, in the moment, responding to basic drives. Animals are unaware of their minds. They are unaware that they have choices to make; they simply make them. Why are we designed differently? Why did evolution inflict non-stop thinking on us?

The critical point: human minds are an evolutionary advantage to the *species* but not necessarily an unalloyed benefit to the *individual*. Minds may make our individual lives uncomfortable, but the human species is successful because we have them. Let's note the things about our minds that have made us an evolutionary success.

- **If we can know or guess what's coming, we can prepare.** Our ability to imagine and evaluate gives us the advantage of anticipating and planning instead of just reacting.
- **If we can understand the "why" of a situation, we can decide how to control it.** Our ability to investigate and generalize gives us the advantage of being able to anticipate the outcomes of new situations similar to situations we have encountered before.
- **"Knowledge is power," and if knowledge is passed on from one individual to another, power can accumulate.** Our ability to communicate with other humans gives us the ability to share useful information in our group and from generation to generation.

These advantages are enormous. For eons, life flourished on Earth. Then in fewer than 100,000 years, starting from almost nothing, we have conquered the world.

Humans can combine experience and knowledge to solve a problem, determine a course of action, or understand a complicated situation. We call this extraordinary human capability "intelligence." We say we think about the problem before we act. We say we study, analyze, or model a phenomenon to predict outcomes. The fundamental human capability we call intelligence is what our minds are drawing on when we "think." Some of us are very good at thinking, and some of us are not so good, but thinking is a fundamental capability of all human beings. Intelligence like ours is a phenomenon that has never before emerged on our planet, and it is our critical evolutionary advantage.

A conversation about mental models

Minds are slippery. Nevertheless, we all have minds, and we all more-or-less know what we mean when we hear or use the word. A mind is infinitely complex, with its workings continually evolving and adapting to the needs of the moment. This complexity makes it hard to grasp and hard to discuss. It's useful, though, to think about a mind having parts and functions so that we can talk about how it works. As we learn about the mind's parts and functions, we acquire essential information that represents the things and processes of the mind. Taken together, this collection of information is what we call a mental model of the mind, and the thesis of this book is *a suitable mental model of mind leads to better thinking*.

We've been using the term "mental model" freely so far, but just so we're all on the same page, let's examine the idea a little more closely. Here's another dialog with our five year-old friend Bobby.

T. Do you know what this is?

S. An airplane.

T. Is it a real airplane? Can you get inside it and fly somewhere?

S. Well, no. It's a little toy airplane.

T. Right. Good. We call a toy that looks like a real thing a model. This toy is a model of an airplane. So what do we call it?

S. A model airplane?

T. Excellent! A model airplane. Now, okay, what do you think this is?

S. A toy car and a box.

T. Is it a real car? Can we drive home in it?

S. No!

T. So, if the little airplane was a model airplane, what do you think we call the little car?

S. A model car!

T. Yes, super. You got it. Here's a tricky question – it that a real box or a model box?

S. (slowly, uncertain) I don't know. It's little. Maybe … I don't know.

T. Okay, what do we do with a box? We put things into a box, right?

S. (nods slowly)

T. Could we put something in the box?

S. Yes.

T. So is it a box or a model of a box?

S. It's a box!

T. Outstanding! Here's another sheet of stickers.

S. (focused on stickers) These are good ones.

T. Would you like to learn some more about models? There are some more stickers.

S. Okay.

T. Good. Let's look at the model car again. What color is the model car?

S. Blue!

T. Right. Now, can you imagine what the car would look like if it were red instead of blue?

S. (tentative) I guess so.

T. Can you imagine the model car painted green?

S. I guess so.

T. So, you said you can imagine a red car and a green car. Where are they? Can you point to them?

S. (After pondering a little, points to head) I think they're inside me.

T. Wonderful! You're exactly right. The model blue car is in the picture, but the model red car and the model green car are in your mind. We can't see them, but you can imagine them. You have created two mental models! A mental model of a red car and a mental model of a green car. Congratulations, you can make mental models of cars. Can you make a mental model of anything else?

S. (enthusiastic) I can make a mental model of a red airplane too. And a green one!

T. Good job! Here's one more sheet of stickers.

> We can make mental models of anything we can imagine. That's what imagining is, making mental models of the things we think about. My mental models are a secret until I tell you about them, and your mental models are secret too. Our mental models just belong to us, and nobody knows about them until we talk about them.
>
> S. I have a mental model of some more stickers.

This conversation added the idea of a model as a representation of something to an understanding already present, toys. The idea of model expanded to illustrate the difference between real and imagined things, which even young children understand by four or five. Finally, the conversation inspires the realization that models can be manufactured entirely in the mind and are personal and private until they are shared.

Let's check-in again with young Bobby and his tutor.

> T. We've learned that a mind is a part of a person, and each mind has thoughts. Now let's ask a question: does a mind have parts?
>
> S. I don't know … probably.
>
> T. Let me help a little. Is your mind a part of you.
>
> S. Yes. (recites) The part of me that makes me me.
>
> T. Can a part of something have parts?
>
> S. (uncertain) Ahh …
>
> T. Does your hand have parts?
>
> S. Oh yeah, of course. My hand is a part of me too, and it has parts – fingers and knuckles and stuff. So I guess my mind could have parts.
>
> T. Good thinking! You know the names of the parts of your hand. Do you know the names of the parts of your mind?
>
> S. No, but maybe you're going to tell me.
>
> T. Yup, I am.

❧ ❧ ❧ ❧ ❧ ❧

For the reader, the box on the next page summarizes the important points just covered. Each chapter has a similar list of takeaways which, together, summarize the major ideas of the 21st-Century Mind model.

In this chapter, our student has begun an adventure into understanding his mind, his thinking, and the power that makes him super. The next chapter introduces the idea of thoughts and how to think about them.

Takeaway — Basics

- My mind is the part of me that makes me me.
- A mental model is a collection of information representing — in my mind — a thing or a process.
- Minds think.
- As individuals, we use our minds when: investigating, creating, inventing, and innovating; evaluating, and planning.
- In groups, we use our minds to: coordinate and cooperate; compete, conflict, and resolve conflict; and communicate with each other.
- We can learn and remember. We not only react to situations; we anticipate them. We can communicate to each other what we know, what we expect, and what we plan, from generation to generation.
- Our species has been an evolutionary success because of our minds.

Based on image by Collin Guernsey

Chapter 2
About Thoughts

IN THE FIRST CHAPTER, Bobby learned, "My mind is the part of me that makes me me" and he learned that, in his mind, he had mental models of the things in his world. In this chapter, we look at the stuff the mind works with — thoughts.

Thoughts of things and events

Thoughts are information bundles we create when we notice something, learn something, or just think of something. After they are created, these thoughts are stored in our memories. When we think, we retrieve bundles from memory, refine, manipulate, compare, and (eventually) re-store a modified bundle in memory.

Many of the bundles represent objects – balls, birds, and ballet dancers. In addition to objects, our minds manipulate processes or events – batting a ball, watching a bird, dancing a ballet. Some experts call these process-bundles events or schema, but, like the object bundles, they're just collections of information.

Conversation about the nature of thoughts

Scientific tools like **EKG** and f **MRI** make it clear that the brain is very busy with turning its various bits on and off in sequences, in rhythms, and generally in patterns. As scientists watch this busyness, sometimes they can make sense of what the instruments show and sometimes they can't. We would have the same sorts of observations if we looked at the flow of electrons in our computer displays; lots of activity, clearly there are patterns of zeros and ones, but without the special capabilities of the monitor screen, we could never see the pictures. Similarly, we might see the rise and fall of electric current in a telephone, but without the capabilities of a loudspeaker, we would never hear the distant voice. In each case, the physical signaling has to be interpreted as information before it's useful.

For this book, we are going to assume that the electrical and chemical patterns my brain makes represent information that my mind can make use of. Patterns of activity in the brain, information contained in the patterns, that's the information that minds make use of. We call a particular set of that information a mental model or a thought. A thought … the information itself … doesn't look like anything. But we can imagine it. Here's a conversation between Sandy, a nine-year-old, and her tutor after class.

T. Hi Sandy. What's up?

S. I've been trying to explain to my little brother Bobby what we've been talking about in class, you know, minds and stuff. He asked me what a thought is, and I made up an answer, and I wonder if I said it right.

T. What did you tell him?

S. Well, I started with what you've taught me – thoughts are the things we think about. You know, things like ducks and airplanes except just in my imagination, not real ducks or airplanes, just inside my mind where I think about things. But he just looked confused.

T. Did you ask him what he didn't understand?

S. Yes, but he asked what does a thought look like? Does the thought of a duck look like a duck? And how do all those ducks and airplanes fit?

T. Those are good questions. What did you tell him?

S. At first, I didn't know, but then I remembered what happened when I crawled under my bed to find my favorite barrette that fell behind the headboard. It was dusty under the bed, and when I got out from under it, I had fuzz all over my clothes. Anyway, I told my brother that thoughts were like fuzzballs.

T. That's original! Why are thoughts like fuzzballs?

S. Well, first there isn't much to see, just a funny fluff of stuff, and that's like thoughts, isn't it? They don't have a particular shape, and you can't see them. Also, they come in different sizes. And they have different things all fuzzed up together.

T. Okay …

S. Thoughts are like that, aren't they? They don't have a shape, you can't see them, and they're all different.

T. I guess so. Anything else?

S. I told him to look real close at all the different things that were in a fuzzball. The one from under the bed had different kinds of dust, some people hair, some dog hair, some spider web, and a cute little dead bug. And then I told him that a thought fuzzball is all mixed up too. You know, the duck thought-fuzzball has as part of it a yellow fuzzball and a fuzzball for feathers and another for web feet, and like that. Fuzzballs stick together to make bigger fuzzballs and thought fuzzballs stick together to make more complicated thoughts.

T. Sandy, I think you've found an excellent way to think about thoughts, but I'm afraid that calling thoughts "fuzzballs" will be distracting from your serious idea that thoughts comprise a lot of different bits and pieces of information. Would you be willing to try the term thought-bundles instead?

S. Okay, I guess so. I really like fuzzballs, but you're probably right, "bundle" is a little more grown-up. (sigh) So, goodbye, fuzzball. It was fun while it lasted.

A bundle is a collection of different things wrapped up together. Think of a thought as an information bundle. Each of the protruding bits represents a little piece of some aspect of the thought. If the thought is "duck," there are strands for shape, some for color, others for the labels "bird, aquatic, mallard," and so forth. Thousands of strands gather together, representing everything I know about "duck" and all the associations and memories I have of ducks, this duck, and any other duck that I may have encountered in experience or imagination ... a vast number of strands.

Thought-bundles come into existence then change, vanish, or link into other thought-bundles at a tremendous rate – much faster than anything I can perceive directly.

Conversation about information in thoughts

Let's listen in on another conversation between Sandy and her tutor.

T. Sandy, I like your description of thoughts as information bundles. Here's a list of the different kinds of information that might be in a bundle.

- **Things** (e.g. ducks)
- **Processes** (e.g. swimming, doing arithmetic, dying)
- **Labels** (e.g. the word "duck')
- **Qualities** (e.g. colors, textures, smells)
- **Locations** in space, time, or hierarchy
- **Categories and membership** (e.g. "all ducks, tall things, stinky stuff")
- **Order** in time or sequence (e.g. before, after, simultaneous)
- **Feelings** (e.g. fear, anger, disgust)

S. I count eight types of information on the list. Are there any more?

T   Excellent question! The list covers most of the things that might be in a thought, but there is one significant thing left off, which I promise we will get to later but, before we talk about that one big thing, let's talk about the ones that are on the list. Why don't you give me some examples of the first two.

S. Well, information thoughts about "Things" are easy. I can have a thought about a real thing like a bicycle, or a book, or a baby. I can even have a thought about imaginary things that aren't real like ghosts or unicorns. I guess I can have a thought about any kind of thing I can think of ... that's funny!

T. Perfect. What about information about "Processes" — walking or running or talking?

S. That's harder. I guess processes are doing something. I can have a thought about things like swimming or counting or eating dinner. Those are processes, right?

T. Yes, exactly. Those actions are represented in our minds as process information thoughts. What about the next on the list. What kind of information in a thought is a Label?

S. Actually, I'm confused about that. I know that the Label is supposed to be what we call the Thing or Process, but if the thing is a duck and the Label is "duck," what's the difference?

T. Good question. We know that a particular web-footed bird is a duck, but what if we didn't know the name for the bird. It would still be a duck; we just wouldn't know what to call it. The "what do I call it" is the Label for the thing with the web feet.

S. But everybody knows it's a duck!

T. Well, actually everybody knows about the bird with the web feet, and you and I call a duck "duck," but people in France call the same bird Le Canard and in Germany, she's called die Ente. Same bird, different labels.

S. Oh, so one thing can have more than one label. I get it … I'm Sandy to most people, but I'm also "Baby girl" to my father, and "Stupid Face" to my little brother.

T. Good examples, Labels are the information we attach to things and processes so we can name them. The names for things are nouns, and names for processes are verbs. That's the way we talk about them when we are talking about language. Understand?

S. I think so. Is this right? In the sentence "The duck is swimming," there is a thing in the water with the label "duck" (which is a noun), and the thing we call "duck" is doing a process with the label "swimming" which is a verb.

T. Terrific! Information bundles that represent Things or Processes can have multiple Labels. In fact, they can have multiple copies of all the other kinds of information in the list too. The best examples are probably the kinds of information bundles called Qualities.

S. I know, I know! Qualities are descriptions of things. My rubber bath toy is yellow, small, soft, and wet. Those are the information bundles connected to the thing I have attached the label "ducky" to.

> T. Outstanding. You've got the idea of qualities. Can you name some qualities for a Process?
>
> S. Well, the duck could be swimming fast; that's a quality of the duck's Process, isn't it?
>
> T. Yes, we usually attach a label to the qualities of things with a word we call what … ?
>
> S. Hmmm … adjectives?
>
> T. yes, indeed, words that label qualities of things are adjectives. So words that label qualities of processes would be called … ?
>
> S. I know, I know … adverbs!

Thoughts can be reasonably simple bundles or can be extremely complicated bundles with bundles within bundles. Bundles can be connected to other bundles in hierarchies and other more complex network structures. Information bundles are created very rapidly, and they form and reform again and again. Sometimes our attention is directed at an information bundle, and we say "a thought has entered my mind." A "train of thought" is a sequence of information bundles that we give our attention to one after another.

⧳ ⧳ ⧳ ⧳ ⧳ ⧳

Sandy and her tutor have been talking about thoughts. Together they have discussed a mental model of a thought and the variety of information that a thought-bundle might contain. In the next chapter, they investigate where those thoughts come from.

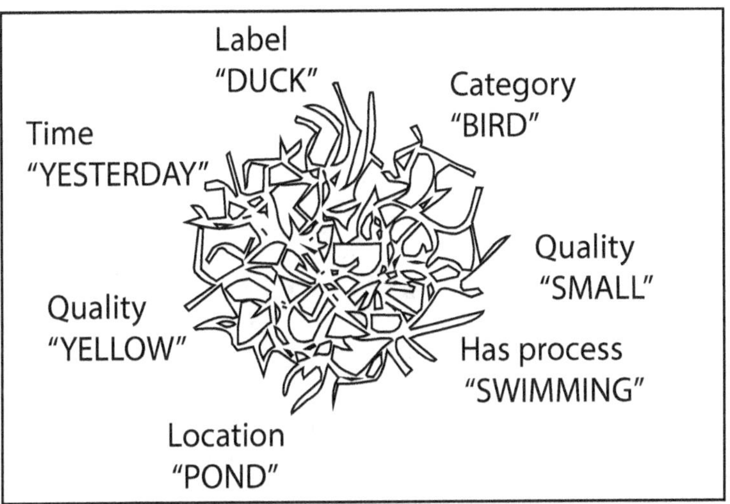

It's impossible to draw a picture of a thought, but this is a simple illustration of a mental model of "I saw a small yellow duck swimming in the pond yesterday."

Takeaway — Thoughts

- A thought is a collection of information in a mind.

- Thoughts represent things, events, processes, and cause-and-effect relationships.

- Thoughts can be simple or complex. Complex thoughts are bundles of simple thoughts.

- Thought-bundles can contain many different kinds of information. For example: qualities like color, texture, or taste; location information about where in time or space; membership in categories, sets, or classes; before or after information; and information about feelings.

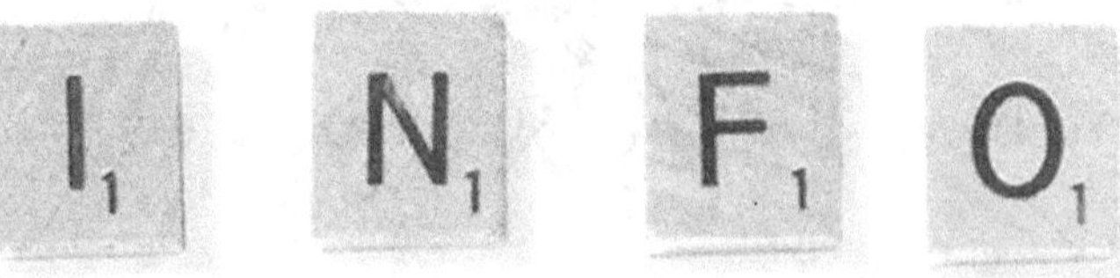

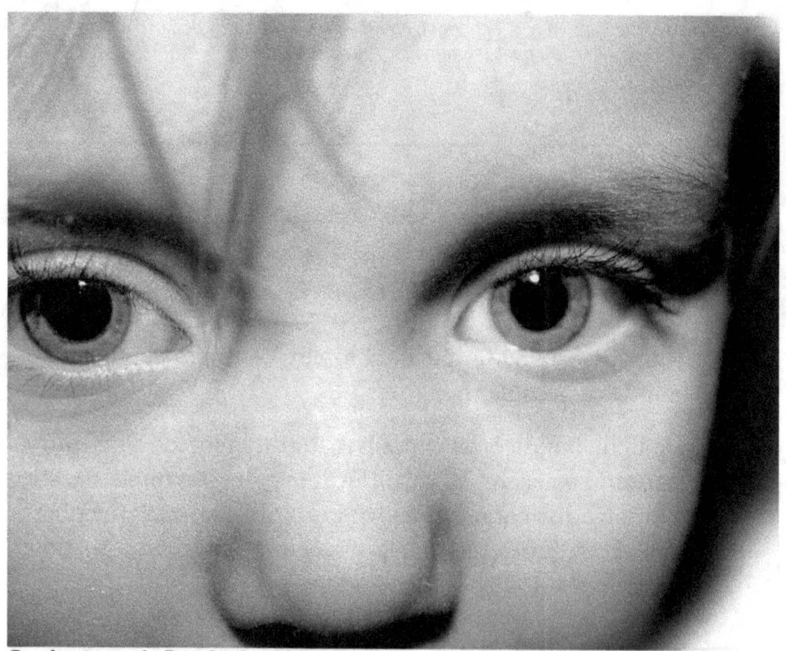

Based on images by Rotorhead and Sarah Pflug

Chapter 3
Perception – Information In

THOUGHTS, IN BUNDLES and bunches, are the collections of information our minds store, manipulate, and consider. In this chapter, we ask the question, "Where does the information come from in the first place?"

Observation about thoughts, minds, and stuff "out there"

Having thoughts that represent reality is a vital part of the mind's power. It's enormously important to be able to hold in our minds thought-bundle models of the "real world" out there; call it REALITY*. Our mental model "in here" (call it "Reality") is how we understand **REALITY** and deal with its dangers and possibilities. We share this power with lesser creatures who have their own version of thought-bundles. My bundles and yours (and probably the dog's too) are different in detail. Still, they must contain enough common information so that we can agree about **REALITY** and navigate the same physical world.

Philosopher Alfred Korzybski got it right when he said, "The map is not the territory and the word is not the thing." Alan Watts, another philosopher, meant the same thing when he said, "The menu is not

---

* In this and later chapters we will use typography to distinguish our mental conception of Reality "in here" from the universe as it really is — REALITY "out there."

the meal." Grasping this truth is fundamental to understanding human thought.

Those bundles in our minds, which we are calling thoughts, are the "maps" and the things they represent are the "territory." It's easy to agree that when we think about "ducks," there are no actual web feet or feathers in our minds. With a bit more stretching, we can agree that our thoughts, which can represent *anything* in the external world, are just mental thought-bundles, not the external realities.

The ability to have some kind of thoughts about the external world is an enormously useful feature shared by all living things. This ability is the essence of consciousness, and it varies from extremely primitive "thoughts" that plants and animals have to the most accurate knowledge of the smartest person.

Humans have built on this basic power and turned it into a super-power by developing the ability to have thoughts about things that don't exist in the real world. We can think about imaginary things like ghosts and unicorns that don't exist in **REALITY**. We can think thoughts about things that aren't external at all, such as our own thoughts and feelings. We can even think about someone else's thoughts or feelings even though we can never know for sure if such things exist. The power to have thoughts about the real world has turned into a superpower that lets us have thoughts about any conceivable world. This is huge!

Our superpower lets our minds hold universes of the large and small, of past and future, and known and unknown. Some combination of thought-bundles represents everything we know or imagine. Our minds accommodate all the thoughts we can think; then, the thoughts create for us an infinitely rich internal "Reality" that is fundamental to being human. Many of our "thought-maps" represent "territory" that has no existence outside of the mind that holds them.

We each live exclusively in the "Reality" our thoughts provide. When we think, we have no choice but to examine and manipulate these bundles – there is nothing else. We can think about anything we can imagine, but we can't imagine anything we can't think about. If the thought-bundle "toy duck" is not available to a person's mind, there's no reason to find the yellow rubber thing bobbing in the bathtub cute or charming.

Most of the time, we aren't aware of the mind's complete subjectivity. Our thoughts make a pretty good map, and we navigate well enough through the physical **REALITY** we inhabit. We become so accustomed to the subjective world our minds create that we forget it's all just a construction built by tools evolved in prehistory. We live entirely in a splendid and very useful illusion. It works so well most of the time that we can correctly call our ability to create and manipulate thoughts a superpower.

We need to add a bit of caution, however, when we engage the superpower. Because we can imagine almost anything, it's certainly true that we can imagine things that are not true, things that don't work the way we imagine, and things that simply aren't real (even if we believe they are). Problems can arise when we lose track of the fact that our thought-bundles don't precisely represent **REALITY** – that our bundle may be a poor "map" to some real "territory" … or perhaps there is no real "territory" at all. Thoughts are inevitable; thoughts are vital; thoughts are great, but … we can't always trust them. So, remembering to be a little skeptical about thoughts, let's take a look at how thoughts get into our minds in the first place.

Conversation about human senses

Sandy and her tutor are getting ready to talk about perception, and Sandy has done some homework.

T. Hi Sandy. Are you ready to tell me about your report?

S, Uh-huh, I'm going to report on seeing, hearing, and smelling.

T. Why did you pick those three senses?

S. These are the ones we mostly talk about, and I could find some information about them.

T. Why do you think seeing, hearing, and smelling are important?

S. I guess because that's how we find out about what's happening.

T. Good, I agree. What did you learn?

S. Mostly, I learned that our senses aren't very good compared to all the information that there is out in the world.

T. For example?

S. Seeing is the most important sense for most people, but the light we see is only a tiny part of all the light there is. It's complicated, but there are all sorts of light that we can't see at all. We don't even think about most of it as light.

T. I think you're talking about the electromagnetic spectrum. Aren't you. That may be a little more science than you've learned yet.

S. I'm not sure I understand it, but I read that other things like heat, and radio, and x-rays are also electromagnetic waves, but we can't see them, so we don't call them light. Some animals can see more of these different waves than we can, but mainly we need special instruments to know they're there. There's lots more than we can see with our eyes.

T. Your information about seeing is a good start. What did you learn about hearing?

S. I learned that we hear vibrations in the air. Sounds are waves, too, but not electromagnetic waves. Sounds are energy moving through the air the way water-waves are energy moving in the ocean. Anyway, we can hear some of the low sounds and some high sounds, but we can't hear every sound. Young people like me can hear higher sounds than old people like you.

T. You're teasing me?

S. Yes, I'm teasing, but you are old, and I can hear better than you. Anyway, there are lots of sounds that I can't hear either, even though our dog and other animals can. Whales can hear sounds that are too low for people to hear, and dolphins and bats can hear sounds that are way too high for us. Of all the possible sounds, people can hear less than ten percent of them.

T. Okay, people can only see a tiny part of the electromagnetic spectrum and hear only a fraction of the range of possible sounds. How do we do with smell?

S. Not so good. Smelling means being able to detect small amounts of chemicals in the air. I read that people have roughly 400 different types of scent receptors, which doesn't seem like a lot, but in combination, we can detect maybe a trillion different scents, which does seem like a lot. But there has to be enough of a smell for us to notice it. Our sense of smell isn't very sensitive. Dogs generally can detect odors much better than we can; some dogs

> are ten million times better than we are. The air is full of chemical molecules, but we can smell only a tiny fraction of them.

T. Wow! You make it sound like people are kind of handicapped. How come if we can't see, hear, or smell very well, we got to be the top of the food chain?

S. Hmmmm … it isn't size or speed, I guess. Elephants and gorillas are bigger and stronger, and lots of animals are faster. It must have something to do with our minds. You know, our superpower thing.

T. Yes, we are at the top of the food chain because of our superpower. Our minds give us advantages that make up for relatively weak senses. The fact is that our human senses got to be just good enough for us to get by in the REALITY we lived in while our minds were evolving.

S. I get it. Our minds helped us learn to do things like make friends with dogs to help us smell things, horses to help us go faster, and stuff like that. Now we've invented machines like telescopes and microscopes that give us senses way beyond what our bodies can do. We can invent these machines because of our minds. That's superpower!

Perception … how information gets in

Perception is the name we give to the flow of information from the outside world into the mind. There is real stuff "out there," and we need to know about it; our lives depend on it. Somehow information about "out there" has to get "in here." That's perception.

Sensory system

We know that our bodies have organs for experiencing the world. Physical structures, nerves, hormones, and electrical pulses combine to provide coded signals into and within our nervous system. We have eyes, ears, noses, tongues, and skin so that we can see, hear, smell, taste, and feel. Scientists haven't agreed on what other senses we have, but they have investigated several that give us additional information about REALITY. See the box below for a recent list.

Science knows a lot about our senses, especially vision. There is a good understanding of how photons are gathered and focused by our eyes, how the photons excite specialized cells in our retina, and how signals are routed through a chain of nerves to various particular sections of the brain that recognize patterns like edges and spaces. After that, the details get murky.

Science knows that our other senses too start with a physical stimulus, code it into a signaling system, and relay the signal into our nervous systems. Ultimately, however, our scientific understanding of the mind's sensory process gets blurry. For example, as we try to trace paths such as the chemicals coming through the air from the oven, into the nose then into the brain, it isn't clear how the fresh bread smell gives us thoughts of home and holidays.

> **The Five Senses**
> - Sight (vision)
> - Hearing (audition)
> - Taste (gustation)
> - Smell (olfaction)
> - Touch (somatosensation)
>
> **Sensory modalities**
> - Temperature (thermoception)
> - Kinesthetic sense (proprioception)
> - Pain (nociception)
> - Balance (equilibrioception)
> - Vibration (mechanoreception)

How do the physical facts of chemicals in the air, reactions in the nose, and electrical signals along olfactory nerves become a memory or a thought? It's a mystery. We add the science that we do know to the parts we don't know and give the mystery a name, "perception."

Perception

The signal flow from the body to the nervous system is immense and continuous. As long as we are alive, our bodies never quit sending information about **REALITY**. Various physiological and brain functions narrow down the information-flow. Eventually, some sense-information is converted into a form that the mind can handle. The conversion is part of the mystery of perception. Nobody knows everything about how perception works, but we do know some useful things.

- Even though we perceive the world as intact and continuous, the nervous system only passes on a portion of the information it gathers. For example, it seems as if our eyes present us with a full panorama, but in fact, we see only a small area directly in front of the eye. The eye continually focuses and refocuses in different places, the visual system processes the information, and ultimately it's the mind that gives us the impression of a continuous, persistent world "out there." (Dragoi, chapters 14 and 15)

- Our sensory system seems to be designed to give us useful information at the expense of throwing away lots of information that is (most likely) less useful. The opposite is also true; expectations in the mind can influence perception formation. (Henrichon 2017)
- In the human mind, information derived from the visual system seems to be more influential than the other senses, at least most of the time. (Rosenblum 2020)
- Sometimes the mind's processing of information can produce ambiguous or confusing perceptions. (Ology 2020) Think optical illusions, for instance.
- Mental focus can have a strong influence on perception. When our minds are busy with one kind of activity, we can sometimes become deaf or blind to sensory information that would otherwise be processed into perceptions. (Chabris 2020)

Probably the most significant thing we know about the mysterious parts of perception is that the information-flows happen almost entirely "out of view." We aren't consciously aware of the details because most of the perception happens in our subconscious mind. Sandy's tutor asks a question.

T. We haven't learned about the different parts of the mind yet, but just from your general understanding of how your mind works, what do you think the most important part of the mind is? Any guesses?

S. Well. thinking is important, but I can't think without thoughts. I get information from perception, but there must have been thoughts in the past, or I'd never learn anything. So — the most important part of my mind must be where thoughts are stored. My memory. Right?

T. Exactly!

❧ ❧ ❧ ❧ ❧ ❧

Perception streams information into our minds nonstop from our first moments until our last. In the next chapter, we see how our minds store and organize those thoughts in memory.

Takeaway — Perception

- There is more complexity "out there" than we could ever know.

- Information comes into our bodies through our senses.

- Perception is what we call it when sense-information is filtered, selected, and recorded in our minds.

- Our senses are "good enough," but not as good as many animals have and not even close to as good as the machines we have built to amplify them — telescope, microscope, etc.

- Most incoming sense information is ignored.

- Our minds work hard to produce the impression that what we perceive is all that is real.

Based on images by Christa Sawyer and Anton Malan

Chapter 4
Memory

As we saw in the last chapter, perception is a brain/mind function that changes external information into thought-bundles. As we encounter **REALITY**, our bodies produce sense-data. Streams of coded information representing images, sounds, and smells flow through our senses into our brains. Once we have the information "in mind," the information is laid down in memory. Our minds absorb the information and "make sense" out of it. The mind lays the new information over the thought-bundles already in memory. The new information melds with the existing information.

Though the brain/mind details of perception are obscure, cognitive science has recently suggested (ScienceDaily 2018) that the activity associated with memory processing is a matter of waves of signals crossing multiple portions of the brain. Duplicate information from familiar sense-data is discarded. Sense-data that contain new information are used to tweak and enhance existing thought-bundles. Sense-data that contradict existing knowledge attract attention or are ignored depending on the context. Then thought-bundles in memory are modified as required.

Conversation about explaining

Memory is a complex, even mysterious, power which we share with other creatures. Still, in us, it is elevated to a superpower because of its profound ability to meld and connect the thought-bundles that make the human lived experience. Sandy sees beauty in the process of memory.

S. I know it's just a picture in my mind, but I like to imagine how perception works with memory. I imagine wave after wave of new perceptions flowing over the existing memory-waves and combining with the ones already there – reinforcing and canceling as waves do – resulting in altered wave patterns that become the new memories. Of course, it's just a silly picture, but it helps me think about how the information gets in and why some information sticks and other information just disappears.

T. That's very poetic Sandy and, who knows, we may find out someday that our brains support perception and memory by doing something very much like that.

S. (smiling) Yup, just thought-bundles on a perception beach.

T. More poetry. Well done.

Now, we've talked enough about ducks and simple thought-bundles. Let's get more complicated. You up for that?

S. I think so.

T. Okay, try thinking about this: why does a grown-up dog weigh more than it did when it was a puppy?

S. (puzzled by the question) When baby-animals, like puppies, get older, they get bigger, and when they're bigger, they're heavier. So, grown-up dogs weigh more than puppies.

T. Good. But there seem to be at least two ideas there. Can you separate them?

S. I guess the first idea is: when babies get older, they get bigger.

T. Can you take that idea apart into some of the simpler thought-bundles it contains?

S. Okay, there's the thought "babies." That's the thought of an animal with the thought "young" attached to it. Then there's "growing," which is a process bundle with "small" and "large" attached in that order.

T. Excellent. Anything else? What about the "heavier" part?

S. I guess the idea is, "when most things get bigger, they get heavier."

> T. So you've got two ideas about babies, don't you? Older causes bigger and bigger causes heavier.
>
> S. Okay, I get that.
>
> T. You used tools in your mind to put the ideas together to make an explanation for why grown-up dogs weigh more than puppies. You constructed a new thought-bundle that explained the relationship of weight to age. Your mind created a cause-and-effect relationship.
>
> S. It was easy.
>
> T. Right, our minds do this all the time. We are always trying to explain why something happened the way it did or how something got the way it is. We can't help it; it just happens. We are continually creating these new thought-bundles to connect cause and effect.
>
> S. Why do our minds do that? Why do we care how things got the way they are? Why don't we just take things as they are and deal with it?
>
> T. Actually, there is an excellent reason we regularly build cause-and-effect relationship bundles. It's a vital part of our superpower. Can you guess the reason? (Pause) No, well. Think about it while we learn some more about how memory works.

What memory does

When I focus on something, that is, when I "pay attention" to a thought-bundle, it's obviously in my mind, but where's that thought when I'm not thinking about it? The answer is, of course, when I'm not thinking it, my mind's representation of that thought is waiting in my memory.

It's become evident to brain researchers that the brain has parts that implement memory. Still, the scientific investigation of the physical details of memory, while interesting, is of little consequence to a person's mind. When we examine the memory part of our minds, we can ignore the biological details. Instead, we can consider our subjective experience. Here are a few of the things that we all know about our memories:

- **We don't remember all of our thoughts and experiences.** How much do we remember? Which experiences are remembered and which forgotten? Why do some thoughts stay with us and others not?

- **Forming memories takes energy and work.** Anyone who has struggled to memorize a poem, a speech, or a part in a play will agree that merely wishing to remember something isn't enough to make it happen.
- **Memories fade over time.** Why do some memories fade more slowly than others? Why do some never fade?
- **We sometimes know that we know something – a name, a word, or how to do something … but can't recall it.** How do we know what we know? Why does the knowledge just pops into our mind a minute, an hour, or a day later?
- **Sometimes our memories are mistaken.** Why do we sometimes recall things, especially experiences, and discover that our memories are incomplete or even entirely wrong?

A significant feature of our subjective experience is that our memory never seems to have holes in it. Our knowledge appears to fill our minds. Only when we consciously seek to recall something … in a test or an interrogation, for example … and fail, do we realize our knowledge is incomplete. We are accustomed to the fact that we forget most of what happens to us, but at the same time, we are confident that our personal history is continuous and uninterrupted. We can thank our brains for the comforting feeling that most of the time, we know everything we need to know.

It seems that the brain supplies us with two kinds of memory[*], short term and long term. Our experience flows continually through our short term memory. That's how we know what's happening now and what just happened. Long term memory is where information is stored that may be useful in the future. The two memories are so intimately connected that we are only vaguely aware of any discontinuity.

Short term memory seems to be organized to provide us with a sense of now. Short term memory deals with experience in time sequence and in list-like order. Short term memory fades rapidly, and unless we make a special effort or the experience has a specially strong impact,

---

[*] Researchers describe a separate third type of memory that holds and transfers information coming in through our senses, but this happens so fast that we can neglect it in our model.

at least half of our memories (even the simplest ones) are gone in less than an hour.

Long-term memory is quite different. The long-term brain-part is comparatively slow. It seems to operate while we sleep as it organizes thought-bundles in complex networks of association such as memories of home, memories of things that are red, or memories of jokes about cowboys. Most long-term memories eventually fade, but some last a lifetime.

We use the brain's long and short term parts in a nearly seamless way to select, screen, and store information. Most of the selection and screening happens without our conscious attention, but we can influence the process by focusing on the information we want to remember.

Information wrapped up in thought-bundles isn't just put in memory and left there like shoes tossed in the closet. When the information is stored, it is first pared down into an efficient size. Then the processes of connecting the new information with already-present details begin.

If we don't ever use the information, it gradually fades, becoming more and more difficult to recall. If we recall the information into our conscious mind, it gets reinforced as we use it and then re-stored in memory. Similar information is summarized, compacted, and stored together. For instance, we don't need to remember the things we see on the way to work each day because, after the first time or two, it's all pretty much the same. We discard irrelevant and duplicate information.

Conversation about memories

Sandy and her tutor are meeting to talk about what Sandy has learned about memory.

T. Are you ready to talk about memory?

S. I think so, but it's a little hard to keep straight what the brain does and what the mind does when I'm thinking about memory.

T. I understand. Cognitive scientists are interested in exactly how our brains do the trick of storing and retrieving memories, and they've learned a lot, especially about how simpler animals do it.

But remember, our focus on the mind lets us avoid the biology of how the brain does it and stick with what memory does.

S. Okay. So, it's all about memory and what it does in my mind. That may make it simpler.

T. Let's start with a straightforward question, "What do we store in memory?"

S. Easy. We store memories. But I guess you'd like a little more detail?

T. Yes, please.

S. At one level, there is another easy answer. We store information coded into thought-bundles, just like the ones we talked about before.

T. Okay, good start. Can you say some more about what we store in memory?

S. There are several different kinds of memories. They have different names. The first one I read about was called "implicit memory."

T. Which is?

S. Implicit memory is information without any conscious effort. For example, as I walk around my neighborhood and dogs bark at me or sniff my sneakers, I remember where the dogs are likely to be, and I get an impression of how friendly they are. I don't try to remember these things, I just do it. My mind and brain cooperate, but I don't notice any conscious effort. This is "implicit memory."

T. Excellent. That's implicit memory. Is there something called "explicit memory" too?

S. Yes. Other information gets stored because we work at it. When I try to remember the capitals of the states or the multiplication tables, a conscious effort is required. This is "explicit memory."

T. Again, excellent. State capitols and multiplication tables are examples of factual information. What other kinds of information do we make memories of?

S. We also make memories of two different kinds of process thought-bundles. Physical habits are one kind … tying shoes or serving at tennis. As I create a new habit, the explicit memory just fades away, and the pattern becomes implicit memory.

Another kind of process memory is information about procedures like doing long-division on paper or cooking a dish from a recipe

I've memorized. This kind of memory is called procedural memory and is also an explicit memory because I have to think about it.

T. You're doing great. Is there anything else? Maybe one more essential category of memory?

S. Oh … let me see. Oh! Yes. I almost forgot the most important part. I store information about what I've experienced! Information thought-bundles accumulate as I live. These are called "episodic memories," and they form my sense of my own history.

By the way, here is a picture I drew of the different kinds of thoughts in memory.

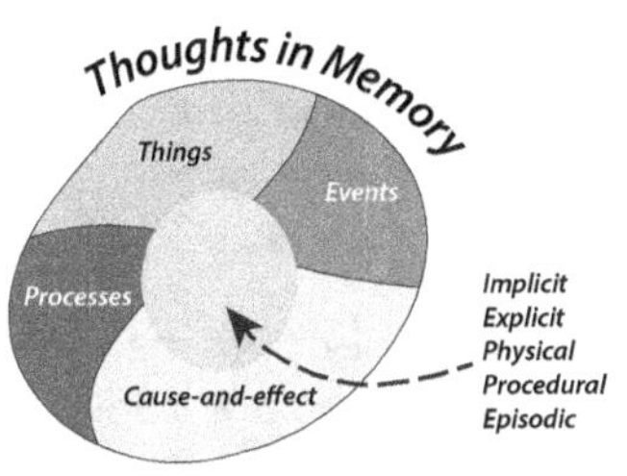

S. My collection of episodic memories is especially personal. They belong just to me. I guess these are mostly implicit memories because I don't make any particular effort to remember my own life.

T. Yes, Sandy. Episodic memory, our personal history, is a story, mostly made up by a mind more interested in a story than in REALITY. Memory takes what it is given to work with – perceptions, reactions, wishes, beliefs, and cause-and-effect models – and makes up a smooth, continuous, seamless story of what has happened to us.

S. You make it sound as if our episodic memories are more like fiction than history. That's a little scary.

T. Nothing to be afraid of, but caution is definitely in order. Memories are thoughts, not facts. It's important to remember that every time the mind/brain combination touches any information thought-bundle, the information may be changed. Details may be emphasized or smoothed away. New information may be added. Information may even be invented to fill gaps. Memories are vital, marvelous, and powerful, but they are not perfect reflections of REALITY and can, sometimes, be wrong. In fact, it's just as easy to remember false information as it is correct information. We must trust our memories, but we must balance that trust with caution when we take the information from memory as the foundation for action.

S. But it feels like it's all true. It's really alarming that what seems so right is so imperfect.

T. We shouldn't be surprised that our memories are imperfect. The wonder is that they are so useful anyway. Memory does it's best to take all the information available and "make sense" of it. Imperfections in the story are cleverly smoothed over. This admittedly imperfect history has boosted survival and become an essential part of the human superpower.

S. Are the other things that we store in memory full of holes too?

T. You may decide that the other functions of memory have some drawbacks too, but I suspect you'll agree that we're better off having them.

S. Okay. What else does memory do?

T. Why don't we make that a research project for you. Come back when you are ready to talk about what other functions memory has besides creating and storing our personal history.

This is a challenging assignment for a young student. Let's see how well Sandy does.

T. Before we get to the details, can you summarize the overall purpose of the other functions of the mind. What's the big picture?

S. (slowly) The big picture is, while information thought-bundles are being stored, memory attaches additional information to them.

T. Good answer; that's true. Why is this important?

S. (with growing confidence) So that we can see how the thought-bundles fit together to make a total picture of our internal Reality.

T. Exactly. The contents of our memories are all we have to describe **REALITY**. The functions of memory that create our internal version of what is "out there" are even more important than saving a personal history.

Can you say some more about the information that's added?

S. Memory puts labels on thoughts. Labels like the ones we talked about are attached when thoughts are stored. Also, information can be added to the thought-bundle to describe the content.

Labels like the word "duck" might be added or qualities like the color yellow.

T. Anything else that might be added as memory is stored?

S. Yes. If there is a strong feeling going on when I have the experience that leads to a memory, then the feeling may be attached to the thought. If I enjoy playing with a puppy, the warm fuzzy feeling gets stored with the memory. If I'm scared by a big growly dog, the fear I feel might be stored with the memory.

T. Good. Attaching feelings to thought-bundles is undoubtedly one of the more critical things that memory does. Anything else?

S. If I notice that the thing I'm paying attention to is similar to another thing I already know about, my mind will probably add a bit of information to connect them.

T. Do we have to notice that things are similar for memory to connect them?

S. Ah … no. I don't think so. I guess my memory can make connections without my thinking about it.

T. Yes, I think you're right. Memory adds lots of information, especially about connections, without our attention. You've studied hard on this, haven't you? Anything else?

S. Oh, yes. I almost forgot. This is really important. I don't think anybody knows exactly how the brain does it, but there are all sorts of connections among all the thought-bundles. We know the connections exist because we can figure out things that require us to somehow know what the links are.

T. For example?

S. For instance. if you ask me to list four animals, each of my thought-bundles for dogs and horses and so forth somehow need to connect to the thought-bundle "animals." Another example (maybe better) is how my memory seems to time-stamp things. I can usually tell you which of two events happened first and roughly when it happened, even though I don't consciously pay attention to the order of my experiences.

T. Good. You've mentioned three of the essential-services memory provides – hierarchies, categories, and time ordering. Memory is very good at making up hierarchies and categories and organizing the specific things we know.

Unless we consciously work at making up categories and hierarchies, most of this happens when we are sleeping. It happens automatically as we learn things and figure things out. It's a beneficial skill, but we don't always get it exactly right. For instance, we can't always tell if a person is in the category "good guys" or the category "bad guys," and we might get confused about whether a porpoise is in the category "fish" or the category "mammal."

We usually do better with time-ordering because it's simpler. Memory keeps things in time order. Can you give an example?

S. I remember that I had breakfast before school and that it rained very hard one-day last week and the dog had to wait for his walk. If I concentrate, I can remember specific times and dates, but mostly I just remember which events came first and which after.

T. There is one more thing, a crucial thing, that memory does. Memory constructs something that helps us investigate and explain **REALITY**. Do you know what it is?

S. Yes, I was going to get to that last. Memory builds cause-and-effect relationships. Memory makes thought-bundles and connections that answer the questions "How did it get this way?" and "What will happen if …?" These are complicated bunches of thought-bundles that explain things.

T. For example?

S. I know that my Mom gets me up and gives me breakfast before she makes breakfast for my little brother because I have to leave for school a lot earlier than he does. The cause is my early schedule, and the effect is I get breakfast first. I must have a lot of thought-bundles arranged as a cause-and-effect relationship to explain that example. I think being able to understand cause-and-effect must be one of the compelling things my mind does.

T. Indeed. This is one of the most potent and potentially misleading capabilities that the brain/mind combination gives us. Our mind really wants to connect events to what caused or causes them. When something happens, we want to know why. We want to understand "how did it get this way" and "what will happen if I do this?" The speed at which we form these cause-and-effect relationships suggests that we have particular brain parts that perform this function.

S. Don't dogs have cause-and-effect relationships too?

> T. Well, animals can be conditioned to respond consistently to stimuli, but it seems that humans are alone in compulsively hooking specific consequences to specific events. The bell will eventually make Pavlov's dog salivate, but Fido will never figure out that it was all the training with bells and chow that made it happen.

Sandy and her tutor go on to discuss how various kinds of information can be associated with a thought. Sandy is making up example sentences to illustrate complex thought-bundles that include location, membership, order, and feeling.

> S. Here's an example about my cousin's wedding last weekend. The first sentence is, "The wedding ceremony took place in the Garden." My memory attached a location, *where* and a time-stamp *when* … in the afternoon. There was also *membership* information. The wedding event (in the category "events") was part of a long weekend, and the ceremony event was part of the wedding event and part of a celebration event.
>
> T. Good start. Do you have another?
>
> S. I made this one up. "The doorbell rang. The dog started barking. I looked up, saw a vampire, and dropped my teeth."
>
> T. Yes, I guess you made that up. What bits did your memory add?
>
> S. Time order. The doorbell, then the dog barking, then the vampire, then I looked up, and then my teeth. I have another one too.
>
> T. Okay.
>
> S. Here's what happened. The cat ran out the open door. I found him in the garbage barrel. He smelled awful.
>
> My memory attached feelings in this example. When the cat ran out, my feelings were alarm, annoyance, and concern. When I found him in the garbage barrel, my feelings were relief and amusement. And when I sniffed him, my feeling was disgust. He was icky.
>
> T. Another good example.

What is learning?

Learning is the process that our minds do to construct our internal "Reality." Every perception is part of learning. Everything we pay attention to adds to our learning. Even awareness of our surroundings and sensations that we don't pay attention to can be part of learning. Knowledge is the sum of all of our learning.

We learn useful things, and we learn things that are not so useful. We learn true things and false things. It's easy to appreciate that thought-bundles (thoughts, ideas, memes, mental models) come in an infinite variety, and some are more useful than others. Of course, the "usefulness" of the learning depends on circumstances. Context matters.

Conversation about understanding

When we say that we "understand" something, we mean that we have stored enough information about the something to be useful for whatever purpose is under consideration. Little kids need to understand cars enough not to step in front of one rushing down the street. Drivers need to understand cars just enough to start, steer, and brake. Mechanics need to understand cars in much more detail to fix them when they fail. The child, the driver, and the mechanic have different information and more and more detailed mental models of the idea "car."

Another kind of "understanding" happens when our instinct for creating cause-and-effect relationships is satisfied. Unfortunately, "understanding" does not necessarily mean understanding correctly. Our minds can get the cause-and-effect link wrong, especially when a simple correlation is mistakenly interpreted as a cause. The rooster crowing doesn't make the sunrise. Clearly, caution is in order when we act on this kind of understanding.

> T. You look concerned, Sandy. Do you have a question?
>
> S. Well, it's just that I understand I need to be cautious about cause-and-effect relationships in my mind that might be wrong. But how can I tell? I don't want to believe something that isn't true.
>
> T. Yes, that is a good question. Actually, we can never be absolutely sure that any particular understanding is entirely correct. You see, the cause-and-effect relationship that a mind holds is always just a model or an approximation of the real complexity of the world "out there." The question gets to be, is this understanding of Reality good enough to be useful to me right here, right now?

S. Still, how do I know?

T. The best answer, I guess, is to pay attention to where any particular understanding comes from. Personal experience is good, but it can be misleading. For instance, we may learn that smiling at people shows that we are friendly, and they will tend to like us. But there are some places where sometimes smiling sends a different message, and people from there may not trust us if we smile.

S. What about the things I've learned from going to school? Do I have to be suspicious of those things?

T. Well, as a teacher, I hope not. We try to make sure that the cause-and-effect relationships we teach are correct and won't get you in trouble. Some school topics are less likely than others to be incorrect. For example, math and science. Other things, especially about how people behave, are much more complicated, and we teachers need to be careful that we explain how much trust we can have in generalizations. Does that help?

S. A little, I guess … but it seems that nothing is quite as solid as I thought, and I need to be careful about what I believe.

T. I think that's an excellent way to think about how our minds work. Next time we'll take a look at the tools our minds use to do their work. Is that okay with you?

S. (slyly) Well … I'll think about it.

ⷭ ⷭ ⷭ ⷭ ⷭ ⷭ

This chapter has presented our model of memory. Next, we introduce a set of abstract tools our minds use to manipulate memories and even create entirely new thought-bundles.

Takeaway — Memory

- We have short term memory that stores thought-bundles on the way "in."

- We have long term memory that does most of the "remembering." It stores thought-bundles, organizes them, and connects them to other thought-bundles.

- Memory stores thought-bundles of several different kinds.
  - Implicit memories ... information without any conscious effort e.g. the day's events.
  - Explicit memories ... information that we try to remember e.g. multiplication tables.
  - Physical memories – "muscle memory" e.g. tying shoes or typing.
  - Procedural memories – patterns of conscious thinking e.g. checklists and routines.
  - Episodic memories – thought-bundles that accumulate to tell the story of our personal histories.

- Memory works very hard to create cause-and-effect relationships by connecting thought-bundles when one episodic memory precedes another.

- "Learning" is adding and adjusting thought-bundles in memory

- "Understanding" means believing we have learned enough to act. For instance, when a cause-and-effect relationship is satisfied.

- Understanding does not necessarily mean understanding correctly.

- Memories are thoughts, not facts.

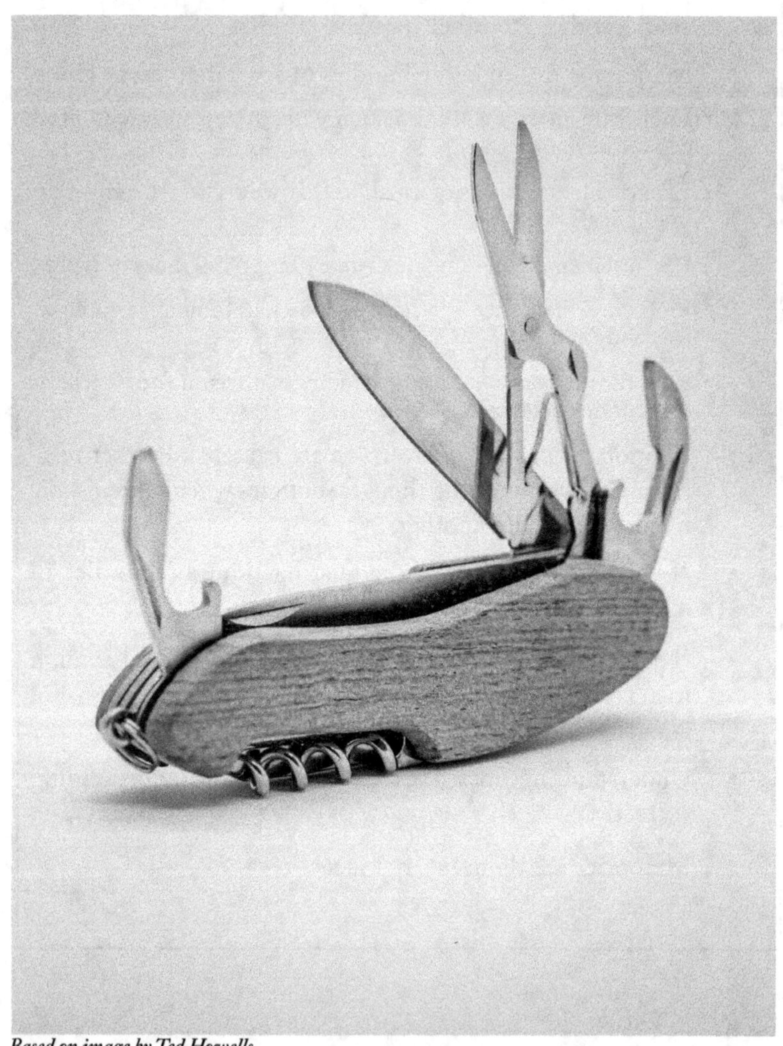

Based on image by Ted Howells

Chapter 5
Mind-Tools

WE'VE SEEN HOW INFORMATION gets into our minds and is bundled and organized into a vast "library" of memories. For our minds to make use of all this information, we have to be able to access it and manipulate it. That's what the mind-tools do.

"Use your head!" We probably have all heard that from time to time. Someone is encouraging me to apply my mind to some situation. The implication is that we have tools of some sort that we can use to reach a conclusion, an understanding, a choice, or a decision. Subjectively we know we have these tools because we use them. We think, analyze, imagine, plan, remember, and "just figure it out."

Obviously, a mind is not a collection of tools in the same way a shop or a factory is, but it is useful to abstract some of our mental processes and explore them as parts of our mind-model. Knowing about them and what they do contributes to improved thinking.

Conversation about mind-tools

Cognitive science shows us which brain parts are active when we use our mind-tools. Researchers are uncovering some of the mysteries of how the tools work, but the details appear to be enormously complex and still not well understood. For our purposes, it's sufficient to call our mind-tools by simple names and imagine what they do.

The Rememberer brings memories to our attention

We recollect those memories which were previously stored. Biologically, recollecting something that has just happened and is in my short-term memory is different from recollecting an older memory that has been saved more permanently as an episodic or procedural memory. Still, for our purposes, we can simply imagine a mind-tool that recollects.

The Rememberer is a tool for my conscious mind; I consciously try to remember something, and eventually, the memory is recollected (or, sometimes to our embarrassment, not recollected). The Rememberer is also a tool for my subconscious; the subconscious can use the Rememberer to just pop memories into my conscious mind. Either way, the thought-bundle from memory wasn't there, and then it was. A complex collection of information that represents an episode, a fact, or a process captures my attention … I recall it.

The Projector resembles the Rememberer

The Rememberer and the Projector use the same brain machinery. But the Projector, instead of remembering something that has happened and been stored away, gathers up a complex set of thoughts and produces a new thought-bundle that represents something that might happen. Like the Rememberer, this tool, too, is used by both our conscious and subconscious mind. We consciously use the Projector to plan something or imagine something. On the other hand, our subconscious also uses the Projector to motivate or frighten us by creating imaginary future events.

The Rememberer and the Projector combine as another key part of the human superpower. Sandy and her teacher are going to discuss why this is important.

> T. Back when we were talking about how the memory is designed to very quickly create cause-and-effect thought-bundles, I asked you to imagine why the mind evolved that way. Remember?
>
> S. Yes, you said it was about our superpower.

T. Now, we've come to a point where we can dig into that question. Ready?

S. Sure. I guess it has something to do with the mind's Projector.

T. Exactly right. As we said, memory insists that there be connections between cause and effect, and the mind/brain combination works tirelessly to create these vital bundles. We are asking for the details of a cause-and-effect relationship whenever we think "why did something happen" or "how did something happen."

S. I get it. A cause-and-effect relation is just a thought-bundle that explains something. It answers the questions about why and how. That's fun. I like to understand things.

T. I know you do. Most people do, especially kids. The mind's Projector tool uses cause-and-effect relations from memory and suggests how events are connected to answer these why and how questions.

S. Is that the superpower thing you mentioned?

T. No. not quite. Yes, it's a fascinating thing to be able to understand how and why things are the way they are. Still, the very super part of the superpower is when the Projector accesses a cause-and-effect relationship from memory and uses it to predict what will happen. Being able to know in advance what will happen is the superpower.

S. You mean like read the future? I can't do that.

T. Can't you? Let me ask a question. What will you do after class today?

S. I'll go home, have lunch, and then go to soccer practice in the afternoon. Ohhhhh … I get it. I'm forecasting the future. But … that isn't fair. I know what I will do because, well, because I'll choose to do it.

T. Okay, here's another question. If it rains hard while you're having lunch, what happens to your plan?

S. Ohhhh … that's a little different. I know that, if it's raining hard, we won't practice because the field will be too muddy. That's a complicated cause-and-effect bundle about field condition and whether or not we can play, so my Projector can forecast that there'll be no practice.

T. Yes, exactly.

The Comparer is the mind's judge

The Comparer answers questions like, "Is this the same as that?" Unlike a simple yes or no, the Comparer judges how much one thing is like another, which of several things are similar, or in what ways things are different. The Comparer sometimes even suggests we examine things that might be similar even when we hadn't thought of them before. Of course, the "things" being considered and compared are the mental-model thought-bundles.

The Comparer can deal easily with questions like "Is a mouse more like a chipmunk or an elephant?" but in some circumstances, the Comparer will definitely need help. For instance, the question "Is a bird more like an airplane or an elephant?" is ambiguous. What is being compared, being airborne or being alive? The Comparer needs context to provide the framework for comparison. Given a context, the Comparer can give answers to many kinds of questions. The Comparer compares:

- **Attributes.** Elements of the mental-model bundles are compared to determine which is more, larger, darker, older, faster, etc.
- **Timing.** *This* happened then *that* happened.
- **Desirability.** What item from a menu do I want? Do I want something or nothing? Do I like *this* better or *that*? Aspects of thought-bundles are examined and compared in light of my inclinations, values, principles, and feelings.
- **Likelihood.** Is *that* really going to happen? Do I remember *this* correctly? Is your opinion better than mine? Is a particular projection or description of reality more or less likely than another?

The Conceptualizer straightens up the mind's "closet"

Conceptualizer makes a new, more abstract, thought-bundle by aggregating more specific bundles. If you make new friends at camp, Jimmy and Johnny, the thought-bundles labeled "Jimmy" and "Johnny" will be added by the Conceptualizer to the bundle labeled "my friends."

Conceptualizer makes new mental model thought-bundles by projecting specific examples on to a more general category. For example, the Conceptualizer creates bundles labeled "Sports I like" and "Sports I don't like" from the bundles labeled "swimming "and "archery" (which you liked} and the bundle labeled "softball" (which you didn't like).

Conceptualizer makes new complex thought-bundles by attaching additional or different qualities to an existing bundle. For example, after a difficult lesson about "lowest-common-denominator," the Conceptualizer might add "confusing" to the thought-bundle. Or, after the first time you pick up an old gold coin, the Conceptualizer might add the quality "heavy" to the thought-bundle labeled "Gold."

The Reasoner is the mind's tool dealing with complexity and uncertainty

The Reasoner applies the other tools of the mind one after another to create a sense of understanding. If the Reasoner follows a path from an uncertainty to a conclusion, we call the process *thinking*. If the Reasoner goes off track and fails to arrive at a conclusion, we call the process *worrying*. If it starts with a specific projected mental target and figures out what additional thoughts and what path would be required to produce the target, we call the process *explaining, proving, justifying*, or *rationalizing*. We use the Reasoner to "figure things out."

The Feeler labels mental models with emotions and "reads" them back

The Feeler is mostly a brain function, but it's also a part of memory operating in support of the mind. Our bodies create the sensations we experience as emotions. The Feeler sticks emotional labels on new thought-bundles as memory creates them. When the memory is recalled, the Feeler reads the emotional label and may provoke the body into manufacturing sensations associated with the emotion. We can't force ourselves to feel a certain way, but we can examine memories and evaluate how we feel about them. Memories evoke feelings, and feelings can also evoke memories.

Conversation about using the tools

S. Can we talk about the Projector some more?

T. Certainly. What's on your mind?

S. I understand that the Projector is part of the mind's superpower because it helps us know what's going to happen in the future, but doesn't the Projector make a lot of mistakes. I know I don't know very much about what's going to happen tomorrow. I can't tell you, for instance, what the newspaper headline will be or who will win the game Friday night. Is the Projector really that important if it's so limited and so often wrong?

T. It certainly isn't perfect, and we certainly would like to be able to tell the future better than we can, but the amazing part is that we can anticipate what will happen at all. This is the superpower. Have you heard the saying, "In the land of the blind, the one-eyed man is king?"

S. (nodding) Okay, so we don't have to be perfect in guessing what's going to happen; we just have to be a little better … but a little better than who?

T. Humans evolved our superpower in the far distant past when we were competing with all the planet's other creatures. We fought for food and survival. Our gradually-evolving ability to predict the future based on what we had learned gave us an edge. The talent didn't have to be perfect; it just had to be enough better than the other creatures.

S. So that's my superpower; I'm smarter than the lions and tigers and bears (oh my)?

T. Yes, that was the start. The result was that fairly quickly (as these things go), we became the dominant species on the planet even though we were nowhere near the biggest, strongest, or fastest. Since then, however, our superpower has become even more important.

S. I don't understand. When we got on top, who did we have left to compete with?

T. For one thing, think about the difficulties caused by the natural environment. We have always had to deal with weather, drought, scarcity of food and shelter. Far and away, however, the big payoff from our superpower has been when we have been competing with ourselves, other human beings.

S. I think we're going to have to talk about that some more. Why should we use our superpower to compete with each other?

T. Put it this way: what is the most challenging, complex, and potentially dangerous thing in our environment?

S. I guess you mean us, other human beings.

T. Correct. We seem to be designed to both compete and cooperate. In groups, we collaborate to compete with other groups. But we also compete within our groups, sometimes dangerously. Sometimes groups cooperate, and sometimes they compete so fiercely that conflict like war arises.

S. It's like humans were designed to keep each other "on our toes." That doesn't seem nice.

T. Your right. It isn't nice, but it does seem to be effective. Effective, at least, for the species as a whole. At least so far.

S. What do you mean?

T. Humans as a group have made enormous progress. First, we mastered our environment and the other animals we competed with. Then we just keep on defining new challenges and conquering them one after another. As a species, we have progressed because of an unplanned but effective balance of cooperation and competition. As a species, we have become mighty because of our minds, but it hasn't always been comfortable for us as individuals. Read your history.

S. But we're getting better, aren't we?

T. I certainly hope so. My generation and yours are the first humans to have to be very careful to maintain this balance. Our minds have given us enormous power to alter our reality – nuclear power, genetic engineering, nanotechnology, intelligent machines. The same power, used thoughtlessly, could destroy us all.

S. Scary! What do we do?

T. We do all we can: think better, think carefully, think of each other.

◦◦◦◦◦◦

We've seen how we can imagine the mind having a set of tools to manipulate thoughts. Next we consider how each person's inclinations influence thinking and actions.

Takeaway — Mind-tools

- The 21st-Century Mind model includes a set of six abstract "mind-tools" that represent the mind's functioning when we are thinking.

- The Rememberer is the part of our minds that brings memories to our attention. We use it to investigate "How did things get to be this way?"

- The Projector does almost exactly the same thing as the Rememberer except we use it to anticipate, imagine, or plan when answering the question "What will happen if … ?"

- The Comparer judges how much one thought-bundle is like another, which of several thought-bundles are similar, or in what ways are some thought-bundles different.

- The Conceptualizer makes a new, more abstract, thought-bundle by aggregating more specific bundles.

- The Reasoner applies the other tools of the mind one after another to create a sense of understanding.

- The Feeler labels mental models with emotions and "reads" them back.

Based on image by Jonas Von Werne

Chapter 6
Inclinations

THINKING DOES NOT take place in isolation. Our inclinations, limitations, and experiences influence our thinking. We each have a unique set of ideas and beliefs that color nearly everything that happens in our minds. We refer to this set with words like personal preferences, foundational principles, and deeply-held personal convictions. These fundamental convictions and inclinations influence the way we interpret our memories and the way we apply our mind-tools. The next few sections look into a way to model and understand how minds are naturally inclined to "lean" in different ways.

Minds are different in many different dimensions

We each have just one head, two arms, ten toes, and so forth. Most features and qualities of being human, however, come with a range of values. For instance, the average British man is 69 inches tall, but 5% are shorter than 63 inches, and 5% are taller than 73 inches. (BBC 2010) If you're not British or not a man, your height will be someplace in a slightly different distribution. Recently no human being was taller than Sultan Kosen from Turkey at 99 inches or shorter than Bahador Dangi from Nepal at just 21.5 inches. (Grossman 2014) The rest of us fall somewhere in between.

The same sort of variation is true for weights, sizes, thicknesses, colors, and anything else we can measure about our physical human bodies. People are all the same in big ways and all different in detail. Physical differences are apparent, but for most of us, the significant differences aren't nearly so obvious, and they are much more challenging to measure.

This book is about minds, so the differences and distributions we're interested in are various dimensions of the mind. Our casual language refers to these natural inclinations all the time.

- "He's very conservative."
- "She's a wild extrovert."
- "They are deeply spiritual but also very practical."

We use this language to describe the general characteristics of a person — likes, dislikes, attitudes, and so forth. We say things like, "That's just the way he is." The language is imprecise, but it's clear that we are talking about something real about a person. We are talking about some real property of his or her mind. In our model, we call these properties *Inclinations* or *Conceptual Balances* and use the terms interchangeably. We call inclinations "conceptual" because they are only useful abstractions by which we label these qualities of our minds. And we call them " balances" because each of us embodies a balance between the extremes of these qualities.

Useful conceptual balances have these features in common:
- They are descriptive of human characteristics we intuitively understand.
- They have a range of variability that has something significant to do with how we make decisions.
- They are (at least in theory) measurable.

We can call them conceptual balances, inclinations, subconscious preferences, proclivities, drives, or personality traits.

Here are six conceptual balances we might describe minds with.
- **Risk-taking/Risk-avoiding** … willingness to accept risk
- **Introvert/Extrovert** … comfort in social situations

- **Leader/Follower** ... willingness to take leadership in group situations
- **Abstracter/Concretizer** ... degree of comfort with abstract concepts
- **Spiritual/Material** ... degree of comfort with spiritual subjects
- **Sustain/Transform** ... degree of comfort with change

Conversation about conceptual balances

Human minds exist in nearly infinite variety. The six conceptual balances in our model of mind are chosen arbitrarily. Other variations in personal inclination may prove useful as the mental model of mind is adopted, taught, and employed in daily life. These six are just a start.

An individual's set of conceptual balances inclines that person to a particular set of desires, behaviors, and decisions that are useful or harmful depending on the social context. Variation in inclinations is a positive for the species as a whole, but may not suit a specific individual or even a small group in a particular context.

There may be some genetic component to an individual's set of conceptual balances, but the balances probably result mostly from experience. Events can change these balances, but in general conceptual balances make a stable and subtle background context for that person's thinking.

> T. So, conceptual balances are like the scenery on a stage: background, sometimes helpful in understanding the action, but not the substance of the play.
>
> S. I think I know what you mean, but I'm a little confused about the part where you said a range of conceptual balances might be good for all of us, "the species" you said, but maybe not so good for an individual. Can you tell me more about that?
>
> T. Okay. Let's look at Leader/Follower as an example. A few of us will naturally take charge in group situations, but most of us will be more comfortable just going along with whatever the group's leader decides. This ratio of leaders to followers assures a group is less likely to be paralyzed in dangerous situations than if too many are trying to lead. Still, it also exposes those who are inclined to be followers to the risk of bad leaders. History is full of leaders who weren't good for the people they led.

S. Is there another example?

T. Try this one. A good balance of Sustain people with Transform people is essential so groups won't get stuck in old grooves when new situations arise. On the other hand, "transformers" may spend all their energy experimenting with new things but neglecting the established things that work. The balance is essential even though there will always be a tension between the sustainers and the transformers. The balance is good for the species, but often the tension is not so good for the individuals.

S. It seems like we humans have evolved to suit the species lots more than each other. That doesn't seem fair.

T. I guess the force of evolution doesn't work so much toward "fair" as it does toward winning the battle for survival. Can you think of something we can do when situations don't seem fair?

S. I hope so. Maybe that's why we have our superpower.

T. Good thought! Evolution doesn't get the last word about our behavior, we do. And the mind has some pretty important parts that help us.

Minds must balance subconscious "kneejerk" decision-making with conscious "reasoned" decision-making. Fast versus careful. The mind's background inclinations uniquely tilt each individual's choices. Across groups of people, inclinations combine and balance the group's behavior.

We speculate that this kind of variation has been an evolutionary plus for humans, but we also note that an individual's inclinations are not permanent. Some portion of our inclinations is likely heritable, but the larger portion is probably learned. We, humans, are very connected to each other, and as attitudes and inclinations shift for the people around us, we tend to shift too.

Large scale changes in the social environment shift inclinations across groups.

❧ ❧ ❧ ❧ ❧ ❧

Conceptual balances influence thinking and decision-making, but only subtly. Other much more distinct and influential contents of the mind more directly guide thinking. These prominent parts of the mind are called a mindset, the topic of the next chapter.

Takeaway — Inclinations

- The 21st-Century Mind model includes a set of six abstract conceptual balances that describe a mind's general inclination and convictions.

- Conceptual balances are subtle influences on thinking that filter knowledge and decision-making concerned with activities like:

  - Taking or avoiding risks.

  - Being comfortable in social situations.

  - Being comfortable with a leadership role.

  - Preferring abstract or concrete concepts.

  - Being comfortable with spiritual subjects.

  - Choosing or avoiding change

- An individual is often not aware of his conceptual balances.

- Conceptual balances may change with experience.

Based on image by Pixabay

Chapter 7
Mindsets and Boundaries

DECISION-MAKING IS WHAT we call it when we choose an action. Unless circumstances change, the action we choose is what we will do. Our actions change things and together we change everything, so we'd better pay attention to how we make our decisions. The universe depends on us.

Just as the physical facts of the universe separate the conceivable from the possible, we have a set of constraints built into our minds that separate the things we could do from the things we are willing to do. For instance, I am willing to shake my fist at the guy who cuts me off, but I'm not willing to force him off the road. I'm willing to tell a polite lie to protect your feelings, but I'm not willing to lie under oath. I'm willing to help you paint your fence, but I'm not willing to pay your kid's tuition bill. Let's call the aggregate of all the constraints in a mind a *mindset.*[*]

---

[*] We use the term mindset differently than some recent popular authors do. For example, social psychologist Carol Dweck distinguishes just two mindsets, "fixed" and "growth," and writes to persuade us that "growth" is better. (Dweck 2006) In this chapter, we use the term mindset in a more structured and value-neutral way.

Mindset, in this book, is the collection of constraints that provide boundaries separating our willing choices from all the other possibilities. We can think of a mindset having parts.

- **Beliefs** are assertions about reality that sufficiently persuade me of their truth that I will accept the risk of acting on them. Most of our knowledge is this kind of belief.
- **Values** are the things that, given my beliefs, I think are important.
- **Principles** are general statements that guide and constrain my choices in some set of circumstances.
- **Rules**, of course, we all know about rules.

Beliefs, a definition

In ordinary conversation, we tend to think of beliefs as abstract things such as religious convictions or faith in country. Strangely, though, we also use the idea of belief very casually in sentences like, "I believe you're right" or "I believe someone is at the door." The fact is that most of us don't pay much attention to what we mean when we use the noun "belief" or the verb "to believe." For our purposes in this book, let's be more precise.

Let's define: A belief is an assertion sufficiently persuasive that a person will accept the risk that it is not true. Note some details:

- A person is required for a belief; trees, rocks, and computers don't have beliefs.
- Several people can "believe" the same thing, but the beliefs themselves are housed separately in the people.
- The assertion can be any statement describing some aspect of reality. The assertion could be expressed as a fact or an opinion.
- If I am sufficiently persuaded, any assertion can be a belief – that is, if I act with confidence that the assertion is true.
- Beliefs are things in the mind ... not in books, songs, or tablets. Beliefs are thought-bundles in the mind.

Beliefs are the granite footings on which our understanding of reality is built.

Core beliefs … not all beliefs are important

Of course, some beliefs matter more than others. For instance, a fan might believe that the Yankees are the best team in baseball and hold that belief with some confidence, but if the team losses the first fifty games of the season, the fan's belief gets harder to maintain. No matter what the team's record, however, a belief about baseball is unlikely to be as important to people as beliefs about the presence of God in their lives or the validity of Einstein's theory of special relativity.

People often talk about core beliefs as being somehow more central, profound, and meaningful than other things we believe. We can get a sense for core versus not-so-core beliefs by paying attention to how strongly they persuade. The more confidence we feel when called to act on our belief, the more we are willing to risk, the more we may consider it a core belief.

If we just sort-of believe something and we're not ready to risk much on the belief being right, we will act with less confidence. Such a lightly held belief might be described as contingent belief. If we don't have much confidence in a belief, but it is useful in some circumstances, it's merely a convenient belief. There is a spectrum from "core" through "contingent" to "convenient" belief.

Where do beliefs come from?

Some of our beliefs came from outside of us, and we generate others internally. Either way, when our memories process an assertion into a belief, we become persuaded that it's true. It's essential to pay attention to how this process of persuasion works.

Assertions come from many directions: other people, books, magazines, media of many kinds, and our own experience. They come from parents, siblings, friends, teachers, from peers and books, movies, TV, and the web, and church, school, the theater, and the local bar. Of course, some sources weigh more heavily than others.

Beliefs from parents

Important people in our lives make assertions of various kinds about the nature of reality, which we store in various ways. When parents tell us things, we are likely to save those assertions as beliefs. For example:

- "Breakfast is the most important meal of the day."
- "Big boys don't cry."
- "Education is the most important thing because they can never take it away from you."

Beliefs from teachers

Education is a hugely important aspect of our culture and a primary distinguishing characteristic of our species. Modern societies have created complex, expensive educational systems to plant thought-bundles in our minds. We don't usually think of what we learn in school as constituting a belief system, but that is precisely what it is. Thoughtful people assert that education is a public good and is central to our behavior as individuals and, by extension, to our success as a culture. This assertion itself is part of our overall belief system.

Our teachers tell us things; they make assertions intended to become beliefs that are stored in our minds. They expect us to learn, to understand, and to believe:

- Fact-oriented thought-bundles like "Three times seven is twenty-one," or Abraham Lincoln was the 16th President."
- Process-rule bundles like "Put on your scarf and gloves before you play in the snow."
- Cause-and-effect relationship thought-bundles like "Rain begins when water vapor in clouds condenses and forms droplets."
- Mathematical mental models like the famous equation $E=mC^2$ or the formula for the roots of a quadratic equation.

Furthermore, our teachers give us practice in applying these beliefs. They teach us to think. Teaching is an awesome responsibility. It's how young humans learn about their superpower.

Internally generated beliefs

We each swim in a sea of communications. Assertions are everywhere and exhaust our ability to digest them no matter how attentive we are. There is more than enough outside raw material for beliefs, but we aren't limited to assertions that other people pass to us. Indeed, some of our most significant beliefs form with little or no specific input from outside.

Professor James Alcock has described what he calls "the belief engine," which he says, "produces beliefs without any particular respect for what is real or true and what is not." (Alcock 2018)

The belief engine can act on outside assertions from teachers and others, or it can run on assertions we just make up on our own. When we do this as a conscious process, we call it thinking, analysis, invention, or some other name for mental synthesis and, by-and-large, this seems to be a good thing. But when our belief engines run without the attention of our reasoning mind, we risk bad outcomes.

Voltaire says, "If we believe absurdities, we shall commit atrocities." When our belief engines are allowed to run without the participation of our reason, absurd beliefs are a terrifying possibility.

Things to remember about beliefs

All the beliefs about reality we hold in our minds are simply assertions we trust. Education is the sum of our beliefs, both what we have learned from experience and what our teachers taught us. Different people believe different things.

- What I believe drives what I value and vice versa.
- In childhood, we accumulate beliefs from adults and educators. As adults, we add our own beliefs through study, investigation, and experience.
- An accumulation of beliefs is called an Education.
- Beliefs have a profound effect on our perceptions, thinking, and decisions.
- We should hold beliefs very lightly until we have examined them carefully.

Our beliefs are all we know about reality and, since reality is more complicated than we can even imagine, what we think we know can only be approximately correct. We would be wise to trust our beliefs only to the extent that they prove useful.

Values

A person's values are the things and ideas that are important when that person is making decisions. What's important? What matters?

If we focus on these questions, we may find it hard to answer. It's not easy to list what's important. It's easier if we are asked to use the Comparer to contrast one thought-bundle with another.

Some comparisons are easy: What's more important, my health or my golf clubs? What matters more, the family dog or the family magazine subscription? Some comparisons are more difficult: What's more important, integrity or harmony? What matters more, democracy or wealth?

It's easy to find lists of values. These lists usually contain nouns (achievement, adventure, competence, etc.) or gerunds (having a family, being around people, working with others). They suggest a quality or condition that we might have, exhibit, desire, experience, or enjoy … lists of things we might want. If we didn't want it, it wouldn't be valuable.

Values are personal

Values are a part of my mind; part of me. We can talk about the values of an organization or a group, but what we might mean by "aggregate values " is difficult to define. We hear statements like "Customer service is a core value of our company" or "Self-reliance is an American value" or "Those people don't put the same value on human life we do." These assertions are fuzzy, and clarifying them (if it's possible at all) would require a great deal of additional complexity. Let's put the vague idea of group values aside.

Let's agree that people have values. To each person, some things are more important (more valuable) than other things. My values are personal. If I tell you what my values are, you pretty much have to believe me. So, values are slippery. They're not just slippery; they're often mushy too.

Values change with context

In a business meeting, I may value quiet-reserve, fair-outcomes, and rational-discourse; I would value radically different things at a prize-fight or a baseball game. In group therapy, I value candor; at a funeral, kindness is more valuable. When I'm out to dinner with a friend, I may value creative imagination, intellectual debate, and good humor; in my doctor's office, I value competence, focus, and clarity.

Another example: In general, I value another person's opinion that I am a serious, competent, mature man. I try to act that way. But, if my grandchild is crying, pouting, or sad, I will put that value aside, put on a clown nose, and act as silly as I can to see her smile again. At that moment, the value I place on your opinion becomes less than the value I put on my granddaughter's happiness.

Values are real

If we agree that values are slippery and context-dependent, does this mean that values are totally shapeless and too changeable to be meaningful? No. Inside this mushy fuzziness about values, there is a core that our minds draw on.

Evidence for the existence of core values is anecdotal but nonetheless substantial. People generally agree about what things are valuable. We may argue about the relative value of home, family, profession, personal integrity, money, freedom, security, health, and personal comfort – disagree on which of these is most important ... but by-and-large we all recognize these things as valuable. Even if one of the things generally-considered valuable is not personally valuable to me, say, having a spouse or a child, I will still recognize that people usually find these things valuable. The things we value, the values we hold, have a lot in common among all human beings. There is something solid in the mush.

Values and needs

It makes sense that the things we need would be the things we value. Abraham Maslow proposed his famous hierarchy of human needs decades ago. (Maslow 1943) Since then, there have been critics and supporters of his description, and several psychologists have extended and modified the original thinking. Still, there is general agreement that, no matter how we characterize, categorize, and label them, humans have needs. The needs fall into two fuzzy groups. We have survival needs, and we have needs that are not strictly necessary to survive as an animal but seem to be essential to survive as a recognizably human person.

Example Survival Needs	Example Human Needs
• air	• some level of security
• food	• human contact
• water	• meaningful activity

Note that needs progress from strictly physiological needs to needs that we think of as properties of mind. Also note that needs progress from personal and individual to relational and social.

We value qualities in ourselves and each other that tend to help us meet our human needs. We call actions to improve the likelihood that we will satisfy needs, virtues. Those actions that diminish the likelihood of satisfying needs, we call vices. Though there seems to be some variation among human societies about the details of virtues and vices, Donald Brown's work on human universals (Brown 1991) is pretty good evidence that all human societies have a large set of common virtues and vices.

Psychologists have surveyed key values not just across cultures but across human history. (Park 2006) According to them, there are six fundamental virtues across all cultures and historical time-periods:

- **Wisdom** (curiosity, love of learning, judgment, ingenuity, social intelligence, and perspective)
- **Courage** (valor, perseverance, and integrity)
- **Love and Humanity** (kindness, generosity, nurturance, and the capacity to love and be loved)
- **Temperance** (modesty, humility, self-control, prudence, and caution)
- **Justice** (good citizenship, fairness, loyalty, teamwork, and humane leadership)
- **Transcendence** (appreciation of beauty, gratitude, hope, spirituality, forgiveness, humor, and zest)

Since humans have needs and humans have virtues and vices, we conclude that in-between the needs and the actions is a set of values that we share and, because the details vary, there are probably also values that we don't share. Either way, there is something in our minds that keeps track of what we value, what's important. These values play a part in our decision-making as well as our broad understanding of reality.

From belief to action

We don't just believe things and that's the end of it. Beliefs lead to customs, rules, and laws. Individuals have different beliefs, but rules, customs, laws, and so forth emerge in groups to implement the group's broadly shared beliefs. Bottom line: beliefs affect choices and decisions. Hence, what a person believes directly relates to what that person will do. It seems reasonable to suggest, then, that the mindset impacts outcomes, and some beliefs will produce better results than others. We've said that beliefs are the assertions we trust are true, and values are the things we think are important. When we contemplate taking some action, these beliefs and values become the drivers of our decision-making; they point the direction in which we wish to take our actions.

Of course, we must consider not just what we desire, but what is possible. Our understanding of reality is an indispensable part of our decision making. Mental models and other thought-bundles are our understanding of how things work, and they are the raw material for our understanding of reality. We have mental models of the aspects of reality in which we live. Inside this reality, our minds do what minds do – we think – and then we take action.

From desire to intention

Moment-by-moment, our minds generate possible actions. This activity takes place internally. Except for the few who are watching with an fMRI, nothing much seems to happen. But we know that we choose the specific action we will take from all of the infinite variety of choices available. Then (sometimes in milliseconds, sometimes after days of pondering) we decide, we choose an option, we form an *intention*.

Intention formation must happen before any action is taken. Recent investigation into this "deciding" process has revealed that it can be underway and may even be complete before I am consciously aware that it's happening. (Wieber 2015) Nonetheless, an intention is formed. For infants, there is probably very little mental activity between "I want" and whatever action the infant takes to get that want satisfied. As the child develops, intention formation gradually becomes more complex, and as adults, we should have a much more extensive, mature process available to choose actions.

The mind could form an intention to start any possible action in the next moment. It might even form an intention to do something impossible. Intentions have an enormous scope. Before we choose an action, we narrow down the choices with a variety of filters.

Initial filtering is done simply by applying the right mental model to the relevant situation. For instance, if a person is in New York and needs to be in London, the applicable mental models of transportation help rule out driving or taking a train. If the person needs to be there tomorrow, the mind quickly can also rule out taking a boat.

Our mental models provide most of the structure of our understanding of reality and limit consideration of intentions to what we call "realistic" alternatives. This application of constraints is straightforward and mechanical. We can imagine a computer making decisions with these kinds of constraints. We might call this the process "analysis."

There's more to the human mind's decision process, however, than analysis. We call the something extra "judgment. " Where does judgment come from, and how is it applied? Beliefs and the values they lead to are fundamental to all our decisions and choices but, by themselves, are not very specific and are not usually clear enough to provide day-to-day moment-to-moment guidance. Beliefs and values set a direction for action, but another layer is needed to help us select the details.

Principles ... the mind's guardrails

Judgment comes as we consider all that we *might* do and focus narrowly on what we are *willing* to do. This narrowed focus involves applying *principles*. Principles are the constraints that reflect our values and apply to our choices – guardrails that keep our actions within acceptable bounds.

Principles are a part of our minds. Principles obviously aren't neatly-written-out statements, but what would they look like if they were? Formalizing principles can be difficult but highly rewarding. Experience suggests that putting principles on paper is a useful way to clarify our thinking about any subject. Let's look at formalizing principles to get a fuller understanding of how they work.

Formalizing principles

A principle is a useful statement of how we will constrain our behavior in a situation. For instance, a driver might have a *rolling-stop* principle: "When driving, I will come to a complete stop at a stop sign unless I can see clearly that there is no cross traffic." This is a principle. It applies to a specific situation (driving, stop sign, etc.), and it constrains our behavior. For a contrary example, consider the simple *drive-safe* statement, "I will drive safely." This is not a useful principle statement … too fuzzy and not a meaningful constraint.

One good test of a principle is to state its reverse and see if the opposite statement is a reasonable principle. In the *drive-safe* example, the reverse might be "I will drive recklessly." No one is likely to constrain their behavior in this bizarre way, so we probably reject "I will drive safely" as a principle. Notice that the *rolling-stop* principle might have a reverse like this: "When driving, I will come to a complete stop at a stop sign even if I can see clearly that there is no cross traffic." This is more constraining, but it is also a principle.

We can say a few general things about principles.

- **Principles are context-sensitive.** In jurisprudence, "Hearsay is not evidence and must be ignored." This is a perfectly good principle in a courtroom, but it is absurdly inappropriate at a cocktail party.
- **Principles can conflict.** We might hold both the principles "I will obey the law" and "I will do whatever it takes to feed my family." When principles conflict, we may consciously try to clarify a situation by fine-tuning the context. For instance, "I will obey the law unless I have to break it to feed my family" is a principle considerably more specific than the broader principle "I will always obey the law."
- **Principles vary from general to particular.** A principle can be as general as "I will prioritize my actions as follows: God,

family, country" or a principle can be as specific as "I will never lend money to a friend."

Principles are the guardrails of our minds. They mark the boundaries of what we will and will not do. We may have principles in common with others, but principles are fundamentally personal. They are, however, not the only boundaries that affect our choices and decisions. Additional constraints arise from society.

Principles to rules

There is only a fuzzy boundary between principles and rules. We distinguish principles from rules by saying that, while principles are constraints on our decision-making that we construct for ourselves, rules are constraints on our decision-making imposed from outside. The entire domain of law … from Constitution to tax code to traffic regulations … falls into the rules category. Rules can also arise from our culture; think etiquette, custom, and "acceptable" behavior.

Customs and laws

Humans are social animals, and as long as there have been tribes, surely there have been *tribal customs* — practices which are mutually understood to be "the way we do things." These customs vary from tribe to tribe, place to place, culture to culture, even family to family. Growing up in a particular family, location, and community equips each of us with a specific set of rules. These rules are typically deeply held and vigorously enforced by peer pressure and the community's hierarchy.

When societies become large or diverse, customs are often codified, given the force of law, and enforced by some form of government. History suggests that as communities grow, diversify, and become more complex, laws often multiply. For example, a Torah scholar tells us that there were only 613 laws for the people of ancient Israel (Hecht 2020); now, no one knows how many hundreds of thousands of laws there are for the people of the United States.

No single mind holds all the modern laws. Customs internalized in childhood and principles developed in maturity must do most of the work of constraining our behavior. We adopt principles like "I will abide by the law as long as it makes sense to me, and I will assume that what appears to me to make sense is probably what the law requires." A bit iffy, but useful. A principle like "I will always determine what the law is in every situation I encounter and take no action until I can comply correctly" is probably impossible and certainly a recipe for inaction.

Heuristics and expectations

Mental models of reality and principles perform the heavy lifting in decision making, but we employ some other mental tricks to streamline their work. We simplify our thinking about how reality works with heuristics ... rules of thumb, educated guesses, intuitive judgments, guesstimates, stereotypes, and "common sense." We combine and conflate these heuristics with expectations that spell out what we expect from other people and what we believe others expect from us. Expectations are just guesses or wishes about the future, not rules.

These simplifications of reality and guesses allow us to make decisions in complex situations faster and with less effort. Some, extremely useful in the evolution of our species, have become built-in to the workings of our brains. We use these short-cuts because they serve us by speeding decisions and avoiding paralysis by analysis. A heuristic like "big scary animal, run!" probably worked enough better to become buried by evolution in our brains. Other heuristics are acquired with experience and training. "Control the center of the board" in chess. "Never draw to an inside straight" in poker. If lost while hiking, "Walk downhill."

We sum up the broad set of heuristics that we apply to human behavior and interactions and call it "being normal." This is a fuzzy set of expectations, but behaviors too far beyond their bounds are considered weird, rude, or crazy.

Universe of choice

You've heard someone say, "I have no choice!" No doubt he feels that way, but it's never true. We have more choices than we can imagine. The choices we make, though, are tightly constrained by our knowledge, our inclinations, and our mindset. The illustration on the next page makes this point.

The physical universe puts the only real constraints on our choices by making the rules about what is possible and what is not. Of course, we don't know about all these choices; some are inconceivable because of our limited knowledge and understanding. Also, we can confuse the situation by imagining some alternatives the physical universe does not allow. Our real choices are the ones that we know about and are possible. These are the things we *could* choose to do, constrained primarily by our knowledge.

For most of us, our inclinations and mindset are an even stronger constraint. Beliefs, values, principles, and rules put strict boundaries around what we *are willing* to do. For all practical purposes, our minds set the limits of our choices.

More conversation about the mind

T. We've covered a lot of topics when we've been talking about thinking and the mind. Help me make a list of what we've covered so far. What was first?

S. The first thing: my mind is the part of me that makes me me. I've known that since I was little. After that, we talked about the things we use our minds for. Like investigating stuff and making up new songs and things.

T. Don't forget, we also use our minds to do things with other people.

After that, we talked about thinking. Remember?

S. Yes. We think all the time and our minds have different parts to do the different things we do with thoughts. Oh, and yes! We talked a lot about thoughts being like bundles. I thought that that was sort of funny.

T. I agree, "bundles" is a funny word to use about thoughts, but thoughts are tough to describe, and the word bundles seems to work. After that, we talked about the different capabilities and tools we have to think with. Do you remember some of them?

S. Oh sure! I did a whole report on senses like seeing and hearing, and then we talked about perception. Perception is the thing that minds do to get thoughts about the world started in our memory.

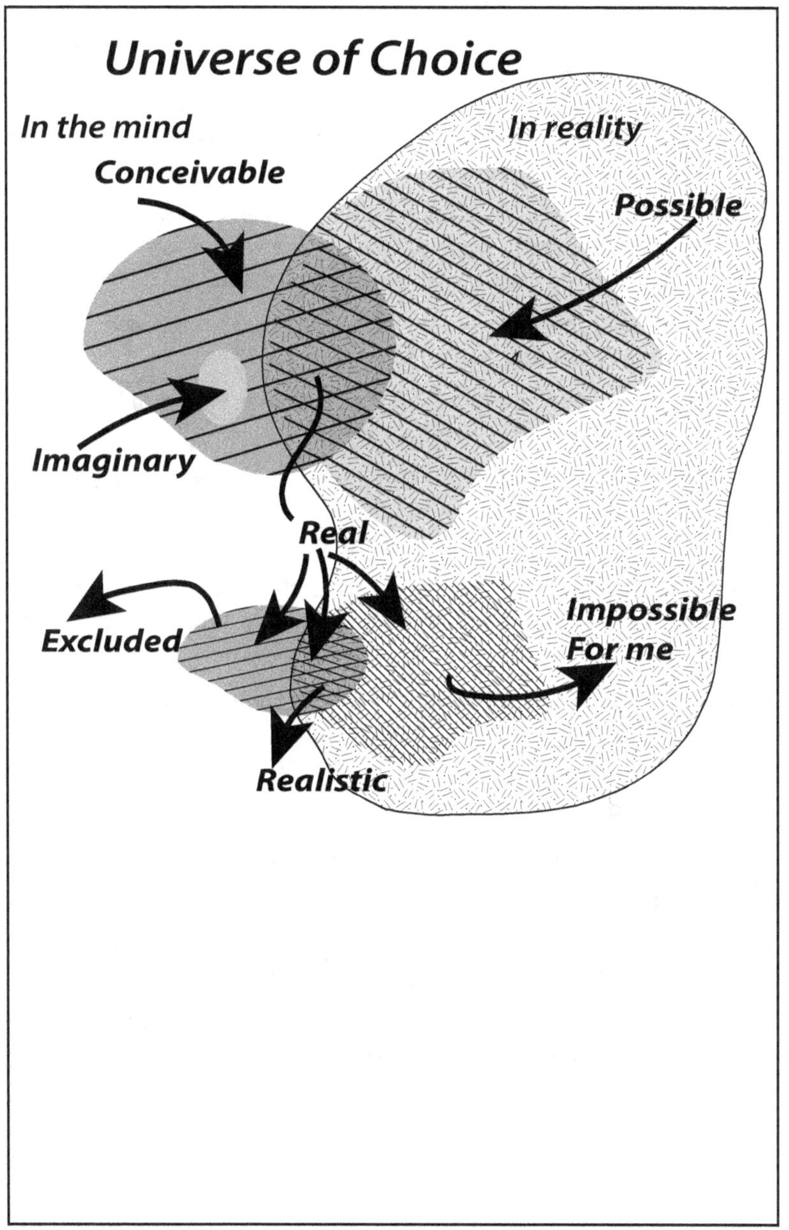

Universe of Choice
In the mind
Conceivable
In reality
Possible
Imaginary
Real
Excluded
Impossible For me
Realistic

Then we talked a lot about memory and all the things that our memories do for us.

T. Anything especially important for us to remember about memories?

S. Well, memory is super important, but we can't always precisely trust what we remember because no matter how much we pay attention, our perceptions aren't perfect, and what we remember isn't likely to be precisely what happened.

T. Excellent. Then we examined what it means to learn something and what we mean when we say we understand something. After that, we talked about tools the mind uses. Like …?

S. The Rememberer, the Projector, the Comparer, the Conceptualizer, and the Feeler. That's five. I forget the sixth one.

T. That would be the Reasoner, the tool that applies all the other tools when things get complicated.

S. Oh yeah. I think about the Reasoner as really doing the thinking, but I guess it doesn't. It's just the part of thinking I like best. I like solving problems and thinking about things.

T. I know you do. You like thinking about thinking. You seem to enjoy abstract concepts more than many people. What would you call that?

S. I'm inclined to be more of an Abstracter than a Concretizer. That's one of my conceptual balances!

T. And after we discussed inclinations, we started in on the part of the mind called the mindset which contains … what?

S. I know, ah … beliefs, values, principles, and rules!

T. Good. What's the mindset for?

S. It makes it easier and faster to make decisions and choices. And it helps the Reasoner tool figure things out.

T. Very good. You've got a good grasp of our mental model of mind. But a few more things are coming up.

❧ ❧ ❧ ❧ ❧ ❧

Guided by our understanding of reality, we choose our intentions. We select from the realm of the possible and, constrained by our mindset, from the realm of the "realistic." Choices remain entirely internal and private until we proceed to action. The next chapter focuses on the bridge from thought-information in the mind to reality "out there."

Takeaway — Mindsets and boundaries

- A "belief" is a thought-bundle representing reality we trust.

- A mindset contains beliefs, values, principles, and rules.

- Everything we call "facts" are actually beliefs.

- Most of our beliefs come from other people.

- We acquire beliefs at home, in school, and everywhere in life.

- Childhood beliefs come from adults and educators.

- Adult beliefs come from study, investigation, and experience.

- Different people believe different things.

- We call an accumulation of beliefs an "education."

- Beliefs influence our perceptions, thinking, and decisions.

- Hold beliefs lightly until you examine them carefully.

- "Values" are the things and ideas that are important to a person when that person is making decisions.

- What I believe drives what I value and (often) vice versa.

- "Principles" are the rules that reflect values and guide choices.

- Principles distinguish what we are willing to do from all the things we might possibly do.

- Mental models, cause-and-effect relationships, and principles guide our actions.

- Customs and laws are rules, similar to principles, that are created by other people.

- Expectations are just guesses or plans, not rules.

Based on image by Bill Oxford

Chapter 8
Change the World

WE HAVE COVERED THE PARTS and functions of the mind, but we haven't said much yet about actually getting stuff done. Thinking is our superpower, but eventually, thought has to be translated into reality. We change the world when thinking leads to intention and intention to action. Action effects REALITY, the reality "out there," and we change the world.

It's a struggle for most of us to accept that our minds wholly construct the Reality we live in. Perceptions and beliefs are the raw material from which our minds manufacture a theater we live in. Experience and common sense tell us that there is something solid "out there." Our personal theater matches up well enough, or we couldn't live successfully in the world. Careful study and introspection eventually convince us, though, that the "Reality" we experience "in here" is not the same as the actual REALITY "out there." It's troubling, but it's unavoidable.

Reality is a mental model of REALITY out there. The more knowledge we acquire, the more accurate and the more useful that mental model is likely to be. Education and personal experience help us expand and improve our model so that our Reality in here matches up better with REALITY out there. When we set out to change something about the world out there, our Reality better match REALITY

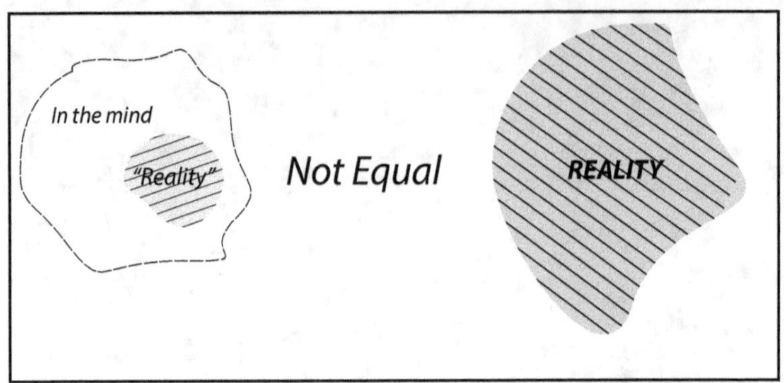

All the "Reality" we experience in our minds is only a tiny blurry made-up image of the REALITY of the universe in which we live.

in a useful way because, whether we know what we are doing or not, our actions change REALITY.

How Do We Make Decisions?

Our decisions are motivated by a desire to change something in the real world. A decision is a conscious choice among possible alternatives … now or later, left or right, fast or slow, him or her, do I or don't I … we think about it, then form an intention to do one thing or another, and then we act.

Decision-making details and the choice of intention depend on the question's structure, on the knowledge we have about the situation, and on our projection of the consequences of the action we choose.

It's complicated. The graphic on the next page gives a sense of the mind's activities as we move from desire to action.

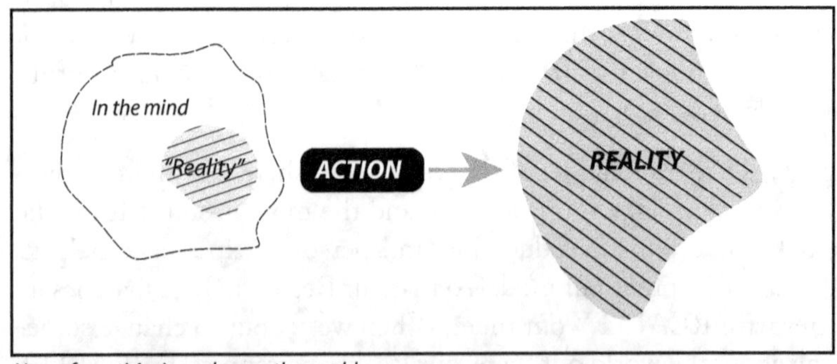

Never forget! Actions change the world.

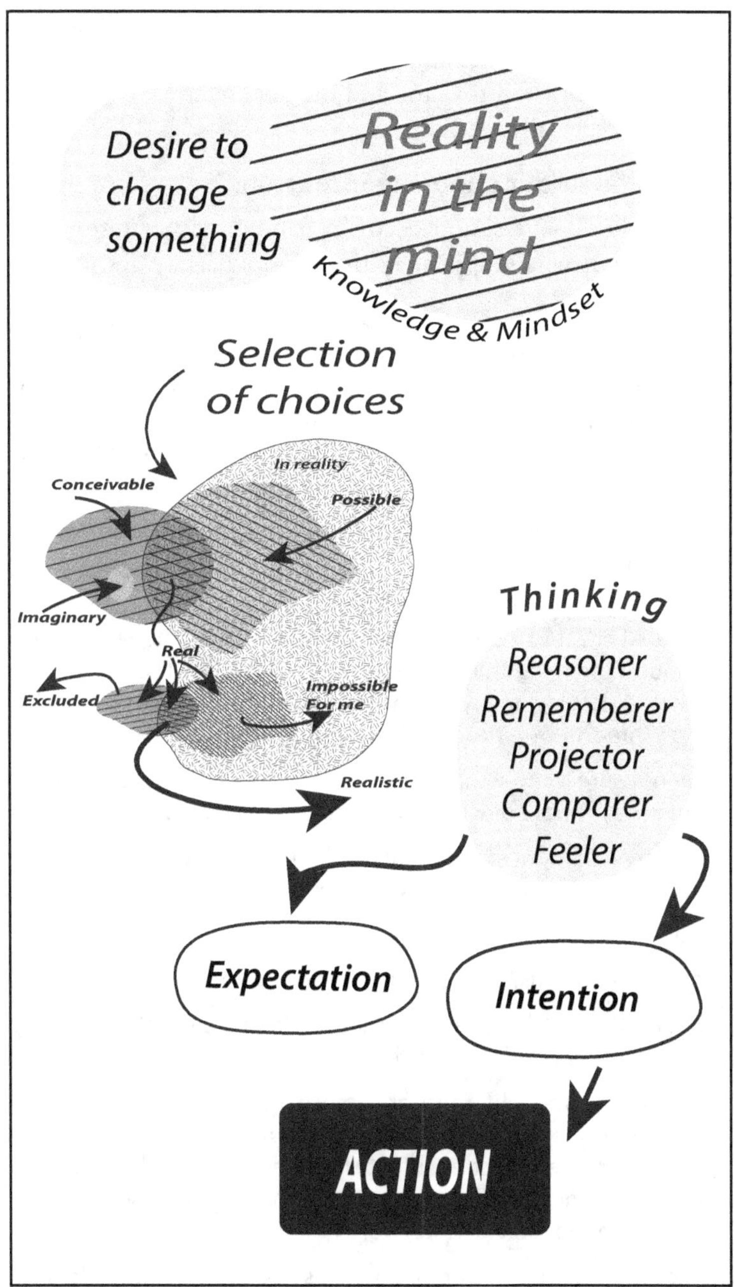

The path from desire to action is a complicated journey through the mind.

At heart, decision-making is the interplay between our situational knowledge and how we use the mind-tools. The feedback between the Comparer and the Projector and our inclinations, beliefs, and principles are especially relevant.

Conversation about choosing intentions

Here is another conversation between Sandy and her tutor. They are talking about what happens in the mind when we are forming intentions.

> T. You've got a good grasp now on the major parts and functions of the mind, but we haven't talked much yet about how we use the mind to make choices and how we figure out what actions we will take. How would you describe what happens when you have to make a choice?
>
> S. I guess I think about the alternatives and pick the best one. Isn't that right?
>
> T. Yes, it is, but your description leaves out some subtle but essential things. Let's start with your word "alternatives" and be very general about it. Imagine that you're just sitting in your room, deciding what to do. How many alternatives could your mind be considering? Three? Ten? A thousand? More than a thousand?
>
> S. I'm not sure. I know that my mind works really really fast, and I'm not always aware of what it's doing. This is a hard question.
>
> T. Let's try a thought experiment and look at some extreme possibilities. Is one of your alternatives to take a rocket ship to Mars?
>
> S. No, of course not.
>
> T. A rocket to Venus? To the moon? To another galaxy, "far far away?"
>
> S. No! That's silly. I don't have a rocket ship, and they don't go to those places anyway. At least not yet.
>
> T. Certainly you're right. These are a few of the things you can think of doing (you just did think about them), but they're not real alternatives. There are, in fact, an infinite number of things that you could imagine doing, but they aren't real alternatives because you know they're not possible. The keyword is "know."
>
> S. I get it. What I know about e.g. helps me separate possible from impossible.

T. That's right. And it's vital. Your knowledge about REALITY is a primary way your mind limits all the conceivable choices you might make. Usually, that process of discarding impossible alternatives happens very quickly. So quickly, we don't often even notice it happening. That's good because we don't waste time and energy considering impossible alternatives. There is a hitch, however. A possible problem. Do you see it?

S. Hmmmm … Oh, Yes! It's about knowledge. If my understanding of e.g. is wrong, I might think something is possible, but it isn't and spend time thinking about potential alternatives that just couldn't happen.

T. Thinking about doing something impossible would be a waste. Is there more?

S. Or, I guess, I might think something is impossible that isn't. Right?

T. Yes. As a teacher, I think that would be the more wasteful thing. I think it's better to "dream the impossible dream" like Don Quixote than believe a task impossible that you might, in REALITY, be able to do. Beliefs matter, don't they?

S. I understand that. It seems like the more knowledge I have, the more accurately I can pick out real alternatives. Is there more?

T. Absolutely. Your knowledge helps screen out impossible alternatives, but they're still infinitely many things you could decide to do. For instance, it's possible to set the curtains on fire. Would you?

S. No! I like my curtains. Besides, I would never start a fire in the house!

T. I'm sure you wouldn't. It's possible, but you'd never choose to do it. You wouldn't even consciously think about doing it even though I've just planted the idea in your mind. A part of your mind would screen it out as fast as it would screen out the impossible options. Lots of screening takes place in your subconscious. Burning the curtains is possible, but there must be something else in your mind that the subconscious selection uses. Do you remember?

S. Yes. You're talking about my beliefs again and about my values and principles. I mean, I believe that setting fires at home is a bad thing because I value my house and family. I have a principle that says something like, "I will only set fires in places where fires should be like fireplaces and barbecue grills." And, of course, there's my parents' rule, "Don't play with matches." All of these things are in

> my mind. And I guess I use them at least subconsciously to eliminate alternatives that I know are unacceptable even if they are possible.
>
> T. All that screening takes place continuously. Consciously and subconsciously we are always choosing intentions for the next moment. And, as the moment passes, we choose again for the next moment. We rarely notice that this incredible mental ballet is even taking place.

Even the simplest choices and decisions involve a tremendous amount of mental activity. Fortunately, we humans are quite good at this sort of thing. The subconscious portions of the mind's activity are extremely fast, and we can rely on them for routine decisions. The conscious mind activity, the part we refer to when we say "I am thinking about it," is usually much slower, but can be much more subtle and thorough. We call this conscious mind activity "reasoning," and we praise it as "reasonable" or "rational" because we know that this conscious mind activity is where our human superiority originates. Reason is the heart of our superpower.

A human mind, complete with conscious and subconscious, encounters the world, explores it, seeks to understand it, and plans to exploit experience for survival. All the thinking that we do is fundamental and essential to survival, but no matter how much thought we give, nothing happens until we act.

Motor System – How We Change The World

Now we ask, "How does thinking turn into action? How does an information flow in the mind change REALITY?"

As we have seen, perception is the function that controls the mind's connection, through the body's sensory system, to the world. Perception is how we get information about reality into our minds. We also have seen that the mind uses its memories and tools to project desired outcomes and make choices. As minds make decisions and form intentions, information flows out toward the world. Only when the information contained in our intention is translated into action, do we act and affect reality.

We humans have a motor or effector system to move ourselves and manipulate things. The effector system is analogous to the sensory system but turned around. Our effector system consists of the nerves, muscles, joints, and tendons of our bodies coordinated through our sensory systems and intentions. Just as the sensory system is the bridge from REALITY to my mind/body, the effector system is the bridge from my mind/body to REALITY.

Every creature has an effector system of some sort; it's the essence of agency. Any animal (plants too, actually) will do what it can to satisfy its needs and desires by pushing and pulling its way through REALITY. We use the effector system to contract and relax our bodies' muscles. We move, gesture, manipulate, and communicate. Most of this activity is autonomic, automatic, or instinctual. We, humans, employ our effector systems in instinctual ways to stay alive. We breathe, eat, excrete, reproduce, and defend ourselves; that's our animal nature. But there's more to "doing" or actually "acting" than an instinctual path from sensation to action. The human mind has an essential place along this path, and, as we have seen, when engaged, we call the mind's output "intention."

Intention is an information-based function of mind that seeks to bring about a future state. The future state, of course, is modeled in the mind. Intention invokes the effector system or ... sometimes when the subconscious portion of the mind has started doing something ... inhibits the effector system and stops the doing. When we say, "I intend to do the dishes," we invoke the complex mental model involved with getting the dishes clean and invoke the effector system step-by-step to carry out actions in e.g. that will bring about clean dishes.

When we must choose, our conceptual balances and our mindsets strongly influence our intentions. Our inclinations and our beliefs, values, principles, and rules are the boundaries within which we shape intentions. We might imagine that we are always consciously aware of what we intend. But in fact, sometimes we don't do what we expect. Or sometimes we do things we didn't intend. What's that about?

It turns out that the effector system is under the control of, not just the conscious mind, but the subconscious mind as well. The subconscious also has access to our inclinations and mindsets and puts boundaries around intentions and influences decisions just as our rational conscious minds do, but not necessarily the same boundaries.

There is a famous experiment involving a marshmallow that tests the will-power of small children. Mother says, "No marshmallow until I get back." Imagine, the little boy wants to do what mother says, but when she walks away, the marshmallow looks very good, and he looks at it, then away, then at it again. The experimenter makes a record of what happens and how long the boy holds out. Obedience is a virtue; do what Mother says is a rule, but marshmallows are so good, and their sweet taste is connected to the marshmallow thought-bundle and associated with a good feeling. Conflicting boundaries and feelings, a very human quandary. (Mischel 1970)

We've seen that our conscious minds may not have a clear idea of the mindset built up during our lifetimes. We rarely consciously examine our mindsets; they just work to limit the mental models of possible actions in our minds. Furthermore, we can be mistaken about the substance or relative strengths of portions of our mindsets. That's how conflicts can arise. We think we want to do something. We form an appropriate intention, but a more deep-seated urge, a more strongly held portion of the mindset, is contrary, and our subconscious forms a contradictory plan. We waver, we vacillate, we flip-flop. Sometimes we just get stuck.

❧ ❧ ❧ ❧ ❧ ❧

The last eight chapters have described the overall shape and substance of the 21ˢᵗ Century Mind model as we experience it. We've explored what consciousness does, but we're only partway done. In the next chapter, we dig into the parts of the mind that are harder to describe and more difficult to understand – awareness, attention, and the subconscious.

Takeaway — Decision, intention, action

- A decision starts with a desire to change something in the real world.

- The desire may be conscious or subconscious, trivial or monumental.

- A "decision" is thinking that leads to an action.

- The thinking involves the mind-tools and all of the boundaries we draw around possible choices.

- The decision involves a projection of how the future will be different after the action is taken — an expectation.

- When a decision has been made and the expectation developed, the mind creates an "intention."

- The motor or effector system is the mind/brain combination that translates the mind's intention into actual body action.

- We employ all our perception-tools to monitor changes in "Reality" as we carry out the action.

- We continuously compare the new "Reality" with the projected expectation and make adjustments with new decisions.

Based on images by Sabine van Straaten and Dakota Corbin

Chapter 9
Conscious and Subconscious

WHEN WE THINK, we are processing information. We recollect information thought-bundles stored in memory, manipulate the bundles with the mind's tools, and refine and save new and modified thought-bundles in memory. All of this activity is information processing. The processing can be casual or intense, trivial or monumental, superficial or profound. Information processing is essential, but from the outside, nothing much seems to be going on. This chapter describes how we imagine the processing of information flows. Let's start by drawing a very fuzzy line through an imaginary house.

Conscious and subconscious

In general conversation, we are not confused when we imagine that things go on in our minds that we don't notice. We call those things subconscious activities, and living inside a healthy human body makes it impossible to deny that such activities take place. How else explain dreams, creativity, or intuition? One simple metaphor imagines that my conscious mind is the main part of the house I live in, and my subconscious is the less important, quiet, dark basement. This metaphor is misleading.

- The subconscious is not a secondary part of the mind; it's at least as important as the conscious mind.

- It may be dark, but it's not quiet; more goes on there than in the conscious mind.

The subconscious is where all the useful bits of the mind are stored when not active. That's where memory lives, where beliefs, values, principles, and all our conceptual balances are stored, and where every thought-bundle resides.

Whenever we remember, project, compare, reason, or conceptualize, the conscious mind recalls bits from the subconscious. The Feeler attaches emotions to memories in the subconscious. Our subconscious continuously monitors inbound information. It filters perceptions and body sensations, then alerts our conscious mind when something interesting or distressing happens.

Outbound information, too, is filtered in the subconscious where our knowledge, values, and principles constrain our possible actions. Finally, the subconscious monitors the sensory feedback associated with the effector systems so that our minds know what our bodies are doing.

Conversation about filters and bias

The tutor decides to introduce Sandy to the topic of filters in the subconscious.

T. There is another wrinkle in our thinking that can affect decisions. Psychologists call this wrinkle "bias," and they've documented a lot of different kinds.

S. I've heard that word, but I'm not exactly sure what it means.

T. Bias is a filter in the mind's subconscious that bends perceptions, memories, and mental models in a specific direction.

S. Like?

T. Well, psychologists have discovered more than 100 different kinds of biases that all subconsciously bend our thinking. I think they are all potentially dangerous, but the one that seems to cause the most mistakes is called confirmation bias.

S. I've think I've of heard of that one. Doesn't it mean just paying attention to new information that supports what I already believe?

T. That's right. Confirmation bias happens when we seek information that supports what we already believe and reject information that tends to contradict some existing belief. It interferes with perceptions, sometimes so much that we just don't see things we don't want to believe. Confirmation bias warps memories by reshaping them into evidence to support some belief. The bias interferes with the Rememberer and causes us only to recall experience that supports a belief we already hold. It compromises the Comparer and puts its thumb on the scale to get a result that supports what we believe. Confirmation bias can be a very corrosive filter.

S. That sounds awful! Ick! How do I get rid of that?

T. A good question, but I think before we answer it, we need to examine the overall role of mind filters and why we have them.

A mind has many information flows. Practically everything that goes on in a mind – such as sensory signaling, perception, memory, or recall … involves information moving and transforming.

We are alive with a ceaseless information flow into and within our bodies, brains, and minds. We can't stop it, and we have much less control over it than our subjective experience suggests.

Filters sitting astride every information flow systematically reshape our perceptions and thoughts; they simplify, tweak, twist, transform, or obscure the information that constitutes our understanding of reality.

All of the mind's filters are there because either we needed them in the evolutionary past or they form part of necessary memory processing. The mind's filters work to speed up and simplify things by modifying information flows in the subconscious. It's easy to imagine why evolution selected for people with faster decision-making brains. A shortcut between perceived threat and action is likely to be a good thing for survival, at least when things are simple (tiger in the tree, don't need to think too long about what to do).

Evolution provided us with these filters because, if we didn't have them, our decisions and actions in unsafe environments would take too long. Without our filters, we would be zombie-slow in nearly everything we do. They serve to make us operate efficiently and effectively in the physical world in which we must survive by shaping choices and decisions. Evolution chose these filters for good reasons, and we should be grateful. We should also be careful.

Back to our student.

S.   It sounds like you're saying that there are good filters and bad filters. Wouldn't anything that messes around with the information in my mind be bad?

T.   Like practically everything that goes on in the mind, whether filters are good or bad depends. If I believe, for example, that people who wear glasses are smarter than people who don't, judgment suffers. Filters like this sometimes keep us from seeing clearly or thinking clearly, and mistakes can be serious; that's bad. On the other hand, when a mother's mind ignores crying babies except for her own infant's unique cry, that can be a good thing. Can you think of other examples?

S.   When I watch sports, it always seems the umpires are calling more penalties against my school's team than against the other school. I guess that's bias.

T.   I imagine it is bias, but it's one we all pretty much share, isn't it … even if it's not fair to the umpires. We'll talk more about biases later. Can you think of a filter that is a useful one?

S.   Maybe this? I like nature shows on TV. Sometimes my brother watches some kid show, and I just ignore it and do my homework, but when the show is over and changes to something about animals, I start paying attention right away. That seems good to me.

T.   Yes, that does seem like an example of useful filtering.

S.   I still don't understand how I can get rid of something like confirmation bias. How can I use my mind to fix a problem that my mind is creating?

T.   It isn't easy, but we can balance the efficiency of subconscious decision-making with another powerful tool gifted to us by evolution. We can consciously examine the filtered version of reality, and we can test it. We can think before we act; this is the gift and burden of free will.

Our student has gone off to think about mistakes and filters and biases. Her tutor asked her to focus especially on the responsibility each of us has to be skeptical of the hasty decisions our subconscious pushes.

Brain and mind interact

Cognitive biology gives us an increasingly good grasp of brain function, and experimental psychology gives us an increasingly good grip on the extent and limitations of the conscious mind, but mysteries dwell in the space between. It's evident that much of the information flow in the mind/brain happens below our level of attention, and we don't know that it's going on. Brains do things, and minds do things, and somehow they are connected. We don't know how the connection works, but we have personal evidence that it does.

The brain and associated nervous system manage functions like heartbeat, hormone releases, and digestion that the mind has little or no control over. My mind can know about these functions, but we don't consciously control them. On the other hand, we understand that some part of my mind gets involved with these things when fear, anger, or cravings – activities in my mind – cause physiological responses. Perhaps a big snake rattles at me. My heart rate increases, my blood pressure goes up, my breathing gets quicker, stress hormones such as adrenaline and cortisol are released, and blood flows away from my heart towards my extremities; I'm ready for action. We can feel the preparation.

The part of my mind that is frightened of rattlesnakes is sending orders through my brain to my body, but I'm not consciously aware of doing it. The part of my mind that is doing it we call the subconscious. In general, what we mean by the word "subconscious" is the part of my mind that I am not paying attention to. When my conscious mind gets involved, I look carefully and see that the "snake" is a length of garden hose, and the "rattle" is a dry leaf scratching along the pavement. Gradually my subconscious gets the message, calms down, and the physiological changes resolve. The subconscious has done one of its jobs; my body has been revved up very quickly in response to a possible threat. I didn't have to make a conscious investigation of my surroundings before I could prepare. Seconds, possibly vital seconds, were saved.

It turns out that a lot of what makes us human happens in the subconscious, so there is no way we can have a useful model of mind without including it. Think of a mahout riding an elephant. The skinny boy up on top is my attention, the conscious mind. My subconscious is the elephant.

Nearly everything my conscious mind can do, my subconscious mind can also do. No surprise here; they use the same brain, same techniques, have the same perceptions, history, feelings, and so forth. The fact is, my subconscious conducts the vast majority of the mind's activity. It doesn't seem that way because most of the action takes place in the dark, so to speak, where I'm not attending to it. Consciousness, on the other hand, is the mental activity that we are aware of.

Conversation about experience, attention and awareness

It's fair to ask, "what is it that I experience when I experience my mind?" The subconscious part is hidden, the thinking details happen so fast I don't notice them, and the mindset and its filters operate automatically. So what is this "experience" I experience?

Subconscious is faster than conscious thinking.

We think at very high speed by using the mind's tools to apply a set of diverse operations to thought-bundles. We are aware of this when we are "thinking about something," but a lot of what the mind does happens below our level of consciousness more quickly than we can be aware of. The subconscious is thinking "faster than thought." Human brains are very slow compared to computers … milliseconds rather than microseconds. But, even so, most of the mind's activities – including the subtle details of the Reasoner, the other mind-tools, and the entire subconscious … take place too fast for us to notice.

Habits and "muscle memory" are carried out mostly in our subconscious, and we aren't aware of the details of what's happening. This fast-reaction kind of thinking is useful for many things that we do, especially as we interact with the simple, physical world, but we need to treat it with caution when very complex or abstract thinking is required. We say, "Slow down and think about it for a minute." When we do things "without thinking," we give up much of our superpower. When our subconscious is thinking "faster than thought," information flows in the mind are vulnerable to subconscious processes that change perceptions, influence memories, and warp thinking.

My attention and awareness are internal experiences. You may guess about my awareness or attention, but I'm the only one who can truly report on it. That's a pretty good way to describe what I mean by awareness or attention. If I can truthfully tell you I am aware of something or that I am paying attention to something, I am. All the things I can report on in that way make up my experience of reality. Awareness is closely connected to attention, but it's not quite the same thing.

Awareness is a hybrid of brain function and mind function. Perceptions like vision or hearing are matched against memory and made into whole thoughts or pieces of thoughts. Psychologists and cognitive scientists have constructed several experiments that prove that I can be aware of something without knowing it. Researchers suggest that there is an identifiable brain part that controls attention by weighing all the present information coming in and letting one piece of the competing bits of information win a kind of a popularity contest and become, at least briefly, the object of my attention. A thought wins the contest and pops into my attention, then other things outweigh it in the popularity contest and replace the previous winner. And so on and so on, very, very fast. (Wired 2018) I know about only a tiny part of this constant activity.

But my parents and my teachers told me, pay attention; they didn't say, be aware. In our everyday speaking, we use these words pretty much interchangeably because attention and awareness have a special relationship. They influence each other. My brain and subconscious mind-parts that do awareness can attract my conscious attention mind-tool, and the attention mind-tool can, in turn, recruit the subconscious awareness mind/brain part to its service. On the one hand, the subconscious monitoring awareness can grab my attention; on the other, I can focus and "pay attention." Awareness and attention reinforce and cooperate. It all happens so smoothly, so consistently, and so quickly it passes without the process itself attracting any attention. I simply don't notice that I am experiencing a constantly changing attention.

Our subconscious does its best to be fast and useful, but it doesn't always get things right. Our conscious mind is much slower but more careful. That's why we pay attention.

Minds turn off like a sunset, not a light switch

We know that our subconscious can be active when our consciousness is more or less dimmed out. For example, when we dream. Recall the elephant; the subconscious part of the mind keeps doing what it does even when the boy up top takes a nap. We know that the conscious part can sometimes be more alert and sometimes less alert. We're bright and fully aware of things sometimes, and other times we zone out, daydream, or even fall asleep. Brain data says the attention-awareness pair keeps working at different levels as awareness fades and, ultimately, only anesthesia (or death) throws a switch and turns both out.

S. What happens to my mind when I'm asleep?

T. Good question. Let's investigate it a little, okay?

S. Okay.

T. Let's agree that while we're asleep, the parts of our brain that run the unconscious things … heartbeat, breathing, digestion, etc. – keep working. Right? So we know the brain keeps working, no matter what else the mind is doing. The mind doesn't shut down and disappear, though, does it? How do we know?

S. I guess I know my mind doesn't disappear, because when I wake up, I'm still me.

T. Good answer!

S. But something's different. When I'm asleep, I just turn off. Don't I?

T. Can you think of anything that happens in your mind when you're asleep?

S. Sure. I dream sometimes. But I don't usually remember what I dream. I sometimes remember some of the dream, but it usually goes away pretty fast.

T. Dreams disappear from our short term memories the way all our sensory input does unless the perception process records the short term memory into our permanent memory. We sometimes remember enough about dreams, especially one that we repeat, so that we can remember and talk about them.

S. I have one of those. I dream about Buffy, the dog I had when I was a little girl. He ran away, and I was sad, but I dream that he comes back, and I find him in my closet or under my bed. That makes me happy in the dream, but I get sad again when I wake up.

T. Can you imagine what your mind is doing when you have that dream?

S. Okay. My mind is definitely using the Rememberer 'cause I know about Buffy and my room and, I guess the Feeler must be working too because I'm happy in the dream.

T. That's exactly right. There are lots of theories about how dreams work and what they're good for, but most people will agree that memory and feelings are involved. One thing we know for sure is that our minds are still working even when we are asleep.

S. I get that. But there's still something different about my mind when it's awake and when it's asleep. I mean, duh!

T. Yes, indeed. Consciousness is the different thing, and we should talk about that.

Conversation about consciousness

Consciousness wields the spotlight of attention across the fields of perception and memory and creates the internal self we experience. Recent thinkers in science and philosophy are proposing radical ideas about the nature of consciousness. They are seriously examining the possibility that consciousness is a fundamental property of all systems. The more complex and integrated the system, the more conscious the system is. (Tononi 2012, Tononi and Koch 2015) A human being – brain and body … is the most complex integrated system we know, and the most conscious.

Remember the slogan *My mind is the part of me that makes me me?* Consciousness is what we experience as our attention shifts from moment to moment. It is our personal movie with sight, sound, smell, taste, and all the other sensations we perceive. We conceive of our experience as this complex movie, and, when we refer to it, we call it our consciousness. In our subjective world, we call our consciousness "I." Our "I" part plus our memory and all its contents – thought-bundles, tools, inclinations, and mindsets – make up the whole of our minds. Remembering the analogy of the mahout and the elephant, we have to be humble about the role that consciousness plays.

Even though we talk about the conscious mind and the subconscious mind as if they were two distinct things, in truth, there is just mind – complex but indivisible and tightly integrated. The experience of having a mind, however, does change. Not from one mind to another, but it changes along a spectrum of attention. David Gelernter has described this spectrum of attention in detail. (Gelernter 2016) Here is a summary of the major points of Professor Gelernter's description.

- Conscious varies along a spectrum, for many of us:
  - Bright, quick thinking, high-energy in the morning
  - Easily distracted, softly daydreaming, low-energy in mid-afternoon
  - Dozing, near hallucinations, at the last edge of wakefulness
  - Finally, total surrender of consciousness into sleep.
- The spectrum of consciousness is universal in humans and is continuous. It varies in range, intensity, timing, and volatility among individuals.
- "Up-spectrum" the mind is concerned with doing (I, myself, am thinking about something). "Down-spectrum" the mind is concerned with being. Turning inward, (I, myself, fade. Being becomes feeling).
- Memory formation is a thing our minds do, but, as we move down-spectrum, we have less and less energy to devote to making memories. Hence daydreams and sleeping dreams are notoriously difficult to recall, and the actions and perceptions when we are in a low-spectrum state are often lost to memory.
- Gelernter says, "There are two fields of consciousness outer and inner. Outer means perceptions of the external world and our bodies. Inner means recollections and ideas we concoct." We frequently and quickly flip back and forth, but outer consciousness dominates up-spectrum, and inner consciousness dominates down-spectrum.
- Up-spectrum, we are acting in the here and now, the present moment, the reality of perception and external phenomena. Down-spectrum, we move into the realm of memory. We can remember what we experienced inwardly, outwardly, elsewhere,

and in the past, but we can actually only be here and now. There is a bright line, but we cross it again and again, often without noticing.

- Gelernter asserts, "Up-spectrum, consciousness feeds memory; down-spectrum, memory feeds consciousness." We may interpret this as there is more information flow from consciousness into memory when we are alert, and there is more flow from memory into consciousness when we are less alert.

T. That's a quick summary* of Professor Gelernter's book about consciousness. I think it gives us some language to talk about your question about what your mind does when you're asleep.

S. You mean my mind is up-spectrum when I'm awake and down-spectrum when I'm asleep?

T. Yes, that's some of the answer, but there is a little more to it than that. He's telling us that consciousness can vary from entirely in charge when we are up-spectrum and wide awake to wholly gone when we are all the way down-spectrum sound asleep. Most importantly, there are lots of stages in between.

S. You mean I can be a little asleep when I feel awake and a little awake when I feel asleep?

T. Yes, and anywhere in between. Remember, we said that consciousness was the lived experience as we pay attention to one thing after another. The spectrum is about how intensely we are attending to that lived experience as it is happening. And there's one more little twist to the spectrum. Can you figure out what it is?

S. Something about being alert?

T. That's the right track.

Alert means that we are paying attention to what's happening around us. However, our lived experience is not just paying attention to outside information; it's also paying attention to what's happening inside, in our minds. They're both lived experiences, but sometimes

---

* Gelernter also provides a vocabulary to describe memories and thoughts. He describes schema in which objects and their qualia and connections are associated in mappings in space or time. He calls these mappings mental *pathways* when we employ them in reasoning, and he calls them *themes* when we use them in less disciplined mental activity.

those experiences are all about the information flow from the outside world, and sometimes it's only about paying attention to things from our memory or the activity of the Reasoner and other mind-tools. Our lived experience, our consciousness, involves both. The spectrum describes how much of each kind of experience we are paying attention to.

> S. So being up-spectrum is paying a lot of attention to my perceptions, being alert?
>
> T. That's part of it, but up-spectrum can also include an intense focus on memories or our thoughts. It's about how much we are focusing, how intense our attention is.
>
> S. You mean up-spectrum is industrious, and down-spectrum is lazy?
>
> T. Sort of, but those are words with value judgments attached. I think it's better to believe that up-spectrum is when our attention is a narrow bright light, and the light grows dimmer and more diffused as we go down the spectrum.

Memory, as Gelernter describes it, is what we casually call the subconscious. Gelernter's concept of memory is more than a simple mechanism for storing and retrieving perceptions. Memory is the active force that creates associations, webs of connections, and abstractions. Memory is what dominates a mind when it is in the lower strata of the spectrum of consciousness. If thinking and "making sense" is what a mind is doing up-spectrum, then feeling and "making stories" is what that mind is doing down-spectrum. Up-spectrum, doing makes logical sense; down-spectrum, feeling makes emotional sense.

This emphasis on memory creates a balanced picture of the mind. In Gelernter's description, "the tides of mind flow ceaselessly from conscious to subconscious and back each day and even within a day."

Gelernter adds an intriguing suggestion. Emotions, he suggests, are the handles or keys that our minds use to organize and retrieve thought-bundles. It seems that the emotions attached to experience combine in complex ways to allow us to call up and associate mental models of both things and processes or events.

No matter how purely rational we may be at our up-spectrum sharpest, we still subconsciously use the "taste" and "flavor" of emotions to fetch thought-bundles from memory, an activity that we are mostly unaware of. This theory of emotion provides a model of how context can invoke a set of filters that our subconscious applies as we select thought-bundles from memory.

In the depths of down-spectrum dreaming, expectation is no longer useful for choosing actions. We are rarely surprised in our dreams. Surprise would require a kind of thinking that is almost impossible when we are asleep. If we experience a projection when we are daydreaming that surprises us, it may be a lucky result of a down-spectrum association that we might not make when fully awake. And if we hallucinate, it isn't weird until it's over. No matter what the level of consciousness, the projecting process goes on, but it's rarely of much practical use down-spectrum.

Gelernter's descriptions also suggest that the connection between thought-bundles and the emotions we use to retrieve them might be at the heart of frantic situations. When we are in an emotional storm, it may seem that we are able only to anticipate the most emotionally loaded near-term outcome.

T. We've talked a lot about the tides of consciousness, as Professor Gelernter describes them. Does this answer your question about what happens in your mind when you're asleep?

S. I think so. My mind never stops, but sometimes I am paying attention to what my mind is doing and other times not so much. Sometimes my mind solves problems, and other times my mind is just the place where I live. Most of what goes on happens without my paying any attention. I can sometimes be very attentive, but other times, my mind wanders. I daydream. Every night I gradually doze off. As I pay less and less attention, my consciousness fades, but my whole subconscious, especially my memory, keeps busy.

T. What does your mind do when your consciousness fades?

S. You said that the brain scientists discovered that there's lots of stuff that happens in the brain when I'm asleep to keep everything functioning, right?

T. Yes, that's the brain stuff that explains why you need to sleep. What about the mind? It keeps busy. Busy doing what?

S. If the brain is sorting and connecting memories, somehow the mind must notice, right? I'm not using my mind when I'm asleep, but if it's still busy, it must be doing something. Is that what dreaming is all about?

T. We don't know for sure, but that's an excellent guess. Brain science tells us that our brains rest a little and then are very busy for a few minutes while we are asleep. The busy times are when we dream.

S. Oh, I get it, I get it! Since my consciousness is turned off, my subconscious can just play with my memories and mind-tools and go off in any crazy direction it wants to. That's why dreams are so strange!

T. Yes, that might be precisely what happens. Especially since we know that emotions get attached to thought-bundles, and the logic of dreams (which are usually very illogical) may actually be the path of feelings as the feeling-connections run through bundle after thought-bundle. The feelings are the logic of the dream.

❦ ❦ ❦ ❦ ❦ ❦

In the last nine chapters, we have surveyed the 21ˢᵗ-Century Mind model, often listening to conversations between a clever young girl and her tutor as they discuss the model and talk about thinking. In the next chapter, we eavesdrop some more as her tutor quizzes Sandy about what she has learned about the mind.

Takeaway — Conscious and subconscious

- "Consciousness" is the lived experience as we pay attention to one thing after another.

- "Subconscious" is the mind's activity we are not paying attention to.

- We speak of conscious and subconscious minds, but there is just one highly integrated mind.

- "Awareness" is the process in which information passes into short term memory.

- "Attention" is the conscious sense of some particular experience.

- Consciousness varies with a spectrum of alertness from "full-awake" to "fast asleep" and all levels in between.

- As consciousness slows and fades, the subconscious mind is more and more in control.

Based on image by Marcos Paulo Prado

Chapter 10
Final Exam

T. Sandy, it's time for our final review of the 21st-Century Model of Mind. Are you ready?

S. I'm a little nervous. There's been a lot to learn. I hope I'm ready.

T. I'm sure you are. Don't worry.

Let's start with an easy one. Okay? What is a mind?

S. Even my little brother knows that one. "My mind is the part of me that makes me "me."

T. Good start. Now, what do minds do?

S. That's easy too. Minds think.

T. What do we use our minds for? What are the important things that we can do with our minds?

S. We each think to investigate, create, invent, innovate, evaluate, and ... eh ... plan! That's what makes it a superpower!

T. Yes, indeed. Superpower. But it isn't just a superpower for us as individuals, is it? What do our minds help us do when we're together in groups?

S. We work together. We cooperate and coordinate the things we do together.

T.   Good start. What mind ability do we have that makes this cooperation work?

S.   Oh … we communicate. We make signals with words, and we share our thoughts.

T.   Very good. Now, do we always work together? Do we always cooperate?

S.   Well, my brother never cooperates with me. We just usually fight over things.

T.   In general, what do we call this kind of fighting?

S.   Competition?

T.   Yes, competition or sometimes, when things are heated and angry, we call it conflict. Given that we do sometimes have these conflicts, can you think of another thing our minds do?

S.   Ah … hmmm … Oh, I know! We can use our minds to resolve conflicts and fix things up.

T.   Very good. That's right. Pretty important isn't it, that if our minds help us fight, they also help us make peace. So those are the activities that our minds make possible.

Can you tell me the essential functions that the mind performs that make these activities possible?

S.   We learned a list. (reciting) Our minds imagine the future, recall the past, feel, reason, conceptualize, and prove. We also learned a list of mental tools that our minds use to do these functions: (again reciting) Rememberer, Projector, Comparer, Reasoner, Conceptualizer, and Feeler.

T.   Good. Let's just remind ourselves that the list of functions and the names and descriptions of the mind-tools are just abstractions that help us talk about what the mind does.

Agreed?

S.   You mean that these lists just simplify a way of talking about very complicated things. People are more complicated than a list of functions, and (quoting) minds are a lot more complicated than a tool shed full of tools. You said that … right?

T.   Yes, I did … okay, moving on.

> When we say that mind-tools act on things, what are the things we're talking about?
>
> S. I guess you mean thoughts. We've been calling them thought-bundles and mental models too.
>
> T. Yes, that's right. It doesn't matter what we call them as long as we remember that these things are all collections of the same thing. Which is …?
>
> S. Information! That's what thoughts are made of … but I like bundles.
>
> T. What different kinds of information can get wrapped up in your thought-bundles?
>
> S. Well, there are information bundles about things, of course. Ducks and cars and molecules. And there are also information bundles about actions and processes, things that happen.
>
> T. Good. Anything else?
>
> S. Other kinds of information get attached to things, information like size and color and texture. Information also gets attached to action thought-bundles … where something happens, how fast, or when it happens.
>
> T. Anything else?
>
> S. I guess the most important other information about something is how I feel about it, so information about my feelings gets attached to the thought-bundles too. I mean, I like the "learning-stuff" thought-bundles, but I don't much like the "tests" and "exams" thought-bundles.
>
> T. I think there is one more important piece of information that needs to be attached to one of your thought-bundles so you can say the answers to these questions. So …?
>
> S. Ahhh … Uhhh … Oh! You mean labels! The thought-bundles have to have names so I can talk about them!
>
> T. Exactly. I know it's easy to forget that we can't talk about things we can't think about.

We can judge from this conversation that Sandy, our clever young girl, has a good grasp of essential parts of the 21st-Century Mind model – the mind's purpose and the contents (thoughts) which the mind contains and works with.

Sandy and her tutor took a short break, but now they've returned and are ready to continue. Sandy's tutor starts into more complicated topics.

T. Can you describe, briefly, how we make decisions?

S. (quickly) Sure. We think about things and choose the best thing to do.

T. (patiently) Maybe describe not quite so briefly.

S. Okay. Based on what I need to decide about, my Rememberer gets a mental model (sometimes more than one) from memory, my Reasoner messes around with the models until it's looked at different possibilities. My Comparer helps me pick the best choice, and then I use the Projector to plan what to do.

T. Okay, that's good. Does your mind examine <u>all</u> the possible things it might choose to do in the situation?

S. No. For instance, there are lots of things I might do after school, you know, the usual stuff like play with friends or go shopping, but there's also a lot of things that I <u>could</u> do like swimming in the fountain at the Mall or painting my little brother bright red that I won't do, so my mind doesn't have to spend time on those things. So my decisions happen faster.

T. How does your mind decide what to think about and what to ignore?

S. Oh, I guess there are lots of things in my mind that narrow down my choices. Let me think a minute.

T. Take your time.

S. (slowly) Well, to start with, my mind can pretty much skip over choices that are just impossible. My mind is full of things I've learned about how everything works, and I don't have to think about doing something that only Superman can do, like jumping over buildings or catching bullets. I think my mind has thoughts, mental models actually, of how the world works, and I usually only have to consider realistic choices.

T. That's a good start. You have knowledge, and the knowledge gives you a head start on picking a reasonable understanding (cause-and-effect mental models) of the situation.

Anything else?

S. Yes, some more things help me narrow down choices. My beliefs are a big thing. I believe the things I've learned and been taught, so I wouldn't intentionally choose to do something that I thought was wrong or impossible. Also, I wouldn't usually want to do anything that went against what I believe is valuable or right.

T. So, you wouldn't choose to do things that violate your beliefs or values. Good. Still, that's pretty broad. Anything else constraining your choices?

S. Yes, there are the rules I make for myself and the rules that other people make that I have to obey whether or not I want to.

T. Can you summarize what all these things in your mind do for you?

S. Hmmm … I guess these things in my mind keep me from making choices that are wrong, stupid, or that can get me in trouble.

T. Good summary! Since you've got all this knowledge and all these boundaries, are you going to make perfect choices every time?

S. Well, no. I make mistakes, but I don't mean to.

T. I know you don't want to make mistakes or get things wrong or have your plans not work out. Nobody wants to make mistakes. So what are some of the things that get in our way?

S. When I think about things – solving a problem or making a decision – the mistakes I usually make are that I don't understand something. Like in math class or when I take the wrong bus.

T. Yes, we make mistakes because we don't have enough information, or the information we have is wrong. Is there anything we can do to prevent those kinds of mistakes?

S. (slyly) Study more?

T. You're trying to be funny, but that's basically right. When we have an important decision (even a not-so-important one), we will do better if we have more knowledge. We correct a lack of knowledge by making an effort to learn things we need to know.

Do you remember what Socrates said about wisdom?

S. Oh, right. Socrates said, "The only true wisdom is in knowing you know nothing." I remember the quote, but I'm not sure what it means. I mean, I do know some things, don't I?

T. You do. I think the point Socrates was making is that the world is so complex that no matter how much we know, our knowledge is only the tiniest bit compared to what we don't know. But we're getting off track, aren't we?

Can you think of another reason we sometimes make mistakes even when we believe we have all the knowledge we need?

S. Yes. I get it. Sometimes we don't see what we think we see. Sometimes we remember things wrong, and sometimes we don't remember things at all. Sometimes the things we think we know are just wrong, but we believe them anyway; when I was little, I thought Columbus was America's first President. When we get things wrong like that, it's easy to make a mistake.

Essay on the mind as a superpower

Sandy and her tutor take another break before coming back for the last part of Sandy's exam. Sandy will undoubtedly pass. Her tutor decides to give her a challenge. The final part of the exam, the tutor says, will be an essay question: In 200 words or less, explain why the human mind is a superpower. Here's what Sandy wrote.

Our human minds are our superpower because we learn, we imagine, and we act together better than any other species.

We have large memories full of complex thought-bundles that hold our knowledge of things and our understanding of how the world works. We learn fast. We organize our experience into thought-bundles of cause-and-effect and a vast web of words, categories, and connections. We never stop learning.

We have mind-tools that recall our learning, help us know what we need to know at every instant, and then show us, in our imaginations, what might happen in the future. We never stop imagining.

We have the power to communicate what we are thinking. We can share memories, we can share understanding, and we can share imagination. And, given this power to communicate, we can collaborate on planning. We make the future together.

All of this might have been created to be automatic and instinctual, but it wasn't. Much of the mind's activity happens in an instinct-like mechanical fashion in our subconscious, but we humans have the ultimate last word. We are conscious, we know we are awake, and we are aware of our minds. We control what we think and what we do. It's just super.

❧ ❧ ❧ ❧ ❧ ❧

Sandy has done a splendid job. We want to teach our kids to think better. We want their subconscious thinking – habits, beliefs, values, principles, and mental models — to be healthy and useful. We want their conscious thoughts to be timely, accurate, as thorough as needed, and built on the same healthy and useful mindsets as their habits.

We want this better thinking for them, but we rarely talk to them about it. If we did try to talk with our kids about thinking, we would probably struggle, we wouldn't have the words and concepts for the parts and functions of the mind ... unless, of course, we do. That's what the 21st-Century Mind model is for: talking about thinking.

You, attentive reader, having reached this point in the book, now have this particular mental model of mind. You and I ... and any other reader of this book ... can now discuss, describe, and argue about thinking. We have a common vocabulary and understanding of the mind's functions because we share a suitable mental model of the mind.

We should begin to teach a model like this to everyone. If we do, our society will benefit from better thinking and fewer errors. If we can talk clearly about thinking, we can learn to think better.

In the next section, we will find Sandy again, this time an older, high-school-age Sandy. We will listen to more of her conversations with her tutor as she continues her investigations into the mind as she and her tutor use the 21st-Century Mind model to talk about thinking.

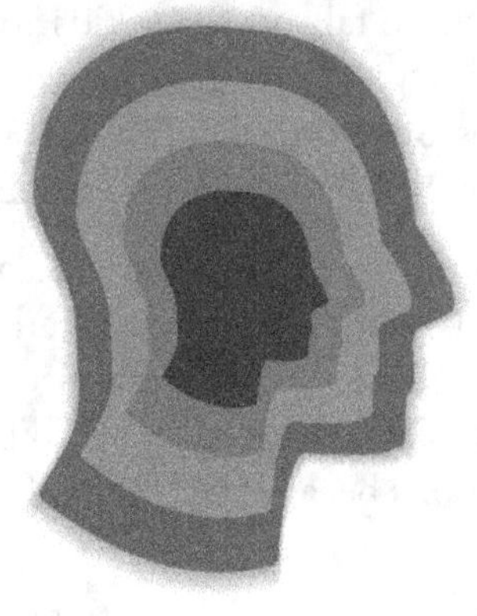

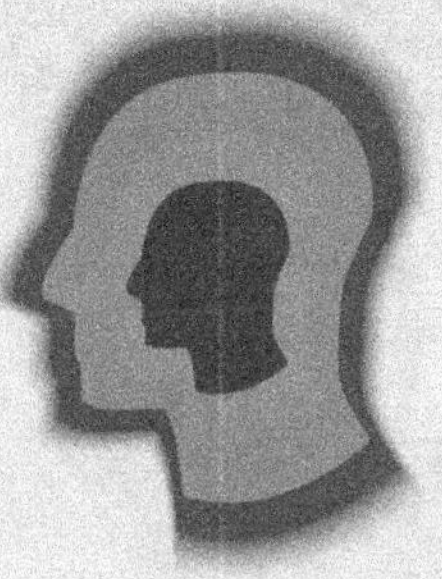

TALKING ABOUT THINKING

Based on images by Casey Horner and NeONBRAND

Chapter 11
Talking About Mistakes

THE PRIMARY REASON for teaching children about their minds is to make it possible to have useful conversations with them about thinking. In this chapter (and the three that follow), we observe Sandy, now high-school age, as she and her tutor talk about thinking. We listen to their conversation and learn along with Sandy. We see how the common vocabulary from the 21st-Century Mind model makes it possible to have clear and straightforward conversations about this complicated subject.

Conversation about making a mistake

S. You got a minute? I've been wondering about something.

T. Sure, what's up?

S. I know it sounds a little funny, but I've been wondering why do people make mistakes. I mean, we always say, "Everybody makes mistakes," and we do, but nobody wants to be wrong. We don't do it on purpose.

T. Wow! That's a great question. Maybe we should take a minute first to make sure we know what we're talking about. Start with the idea of a mistake. What is a mistake?

S. That's easy; it's when we get something wrong.

T. You mean when I break a law? Say I intentionally park at a fire hydrant and get a ticket. Was that a mistake?

S. I guess not. You took a chance, but you did it on purpose, so it wasn't a mistake. I guess part of making a mistake is having something work out in a way I didn't want it to, something I didn't expect.

T. Okay, that's a start. It was a mistake because you didn't get what you expected. Where did the expectation come from?

S. When I think about a situation, eventually my Projector and Comparer settle on a plan because I project a particular outcome I want. The desired outcome is the expectation.

T. So, your mind does some thinking, produces an expectation, life happens, and then poof, the expectation was wrong. That's a mistake, right?

S. Yes, I guess so … that seems right. The reality didn't match my expectation. It would be stupid to say reality was wrong, so it had to be my expectation that was wrong. I guess this mismatch is what we call a mistake.

T. (approving) Okay. Next question. Why didn't your expectation match the reality?

S. Something must have been wrong with my thinking.

T. Yes. Break it down.

S. First, I pay attention to the situation. That's perception and memory working to give me information about what my current reality is. The information comes in the form of some mental model, probably a cause-and-effect relationship, plus whatever context is relevant to what my senses are telling me.

T. Good. Your mind produces an awareness and some understanding that you pay attention to. What then?

S. Based on the awareness of the situation, I imagine the future and how it depends on what I do. Then I decide.

T. Okay. You put all the tools of your mind to work, do some thinking by projecting some alternatives, and pick the one your Comparer judges to be best. You act and (as we said) poof. What went wrong?

> S. Golly, it's hard to say. So many things were involved. I mean, maybe I didn't understand the situation. Maybe my perceptions were wrong. Maybe my memory wasn't exactly right, or I remembered the wrong thing. Perhaps I used the wrong cause-and-effect mental model. Perhaps I just didn't think about the situation long enough before I made a decision. Lots of ways to screw up. It's a wonder I ever get things right.
>
> T. Don't be too hard on yourself. The mind is an excellent tool, but it's just a tool. The Projector mind-tool is only as good as the information it has to work with. And, as wise folks have reminded us, "It is difficult to make predictions, especially about the future."

Sandy is quick to grasp that mistakes result from the mind's limitations. Evolution gave us a finite brain with a marvelous, but not magical, mind. Our experience lets us build models in our minds of the reality in which we live, but the models aren't the reality, just models. The statistician George Box is credited with the observation, "All models are wrong; some are useful." In his writing on the subject, Box suggested that useful models are simple and focus on the essential features of reality the model is trying to represent. When we humans evolved our model-making minds, simple survival and procreation were the criteria for selection. Perhaps, our cultural evolution has begun to modify the criteria in ways that are no longer so simple.

Conversation about the mind's limitations

Let's rejoin our student as she asks about the limitations that we have inherited.

> S. I get it that I make mistakes because my mind has limitations, but why didn't we just evolve a better mind so we don't make so many mistakes?
>
> T. Science tells us that human evolution has been going on for a long time, millions of years. Most of that time, the pressures that worked to influence selection were matters of environment and competition from other species. The jungle and savanna where humans lived was a complex and dangerous place. Human intelligence and ingenuity have worked for several hundred-thousand years to

S. develop cultures that reduced the dangers. The cost of increased safety was increased complexity. Can you think of an example?

S. Hmmm … more complex but safer … Oh, what about agriculture? I mean, growing stuff is more complicated than just killing rabbits and picking bananas. But if we can grow food, I guess life was safer because we weren't so likely to go hungry.

T. That's a perfect example. Human culture began to accumulate knowledge that reduced dangers, especially about hunger. We benefited tremendously from our human ability to imagine, plan, and remember things combined with our ability to communicate with each other and with our children. But the changes in how we lived just kept on making life more and more complicated.

S. So, is this right; when we humans started making complicated cultures, our minds didn't work as well as they did when things were just simple?

T. Not quite. Our minds and brains didn't change much, but the built-in, automatic things that our subconscious does for us didn't match up quite as well to the demands of the more complex reality we were living in. The result is that to survive and prosper, we've had to learn to depend more on the conscious mind and consciously use the mind's tools more often.

S. Okay, I get it. We had to get a little bit more cautious about the "knee-jerk" stuff. But why did we have the knee-jerk stuff in the first place? Oh, of course, I know that. We talked about it. We have the built-in automatic responses from the subconscious because it's fast, and fast is vital when danger is involved.

T. Yes, indeed. As our human efforts changed our environment toward safer but more complicated, human thinking had to start depending more on conscious thought, less subconscious. It turns out that this shift is one of those things that the more we do it, the faster it grows. That's exponential growth. We can easily follow the increase in complexity as cultures and technologies grew from prehistoric times, through antiquity, to the Enlightenment, and modern times.

S. I guess that means that we have to pay more attention now to how the mind works than we used to. Is that why we study this stuff?

T. Exactly! If you were a little kid, you'd get a gold star. Before we leave the topic, however, let's review some more of the details about making — or not making — mistakes. Can you summarize in one sentence why mistakes happen?

S. Ahhh … let's see. How's this: we make mistakes when our minds don't understand reality well enough.

T. Very good. Now, how does it happen that our minds don't understand well enough? I think you can tell me at least two ways that can happen.

S. One way could be that I don't understand what the actual current situation is. My perception can be mistaken and I get the context wrong. Maybe it was dark in the hall, and I thought the backpack was my red one, but it really was my brother's blue one. So I made a mistake. That's one kind of misunderstanding.

T. And another kind?

S. Well … maybe I don't understand correctly how something works, but I believe I do. Like, maybe I believe that you get clothes clean by washing them in the wash-machine and drying them in the clothes dryer, but I don't know that some things like my favorite cashmere sweater have to go to the dry cleaner. Washing my sweater would be a big mistake.

T. How would you describe this kind of mistake?

S. I guess my mental model of cleaning clothes was too simple. I'd need another different model for delicate things like my sweater. Or maybe I'd need a better process model that involved reading the care labels on all my clothes before deciding how to get them clean.

T. Is it fair to say, your model of cleaning clothes wasn't close enough to reality to be useful in the case of your sweater?

S. Yeah, I guess so. When my thought-bundles don't match up with what's real, mistakes happen.

T. Can you think of one more way a mistake like that could happen? What about your mindset?

S. Oh, yeah. The belief part. If I believed my sweater was cotton or I believed that all clothes should go in the washer, I might make that mistake. I guess that believing things that aren't true must be a huge reason people make mistakes.

T. You can certainly say that again!

We call it a mistake when we take action and don't get what we expect; somehow, the physical reality of the universe isn't the way we thought it was or doesn't behave the way we thought it would. Fundamental sources of mistakes are believing things that aren't true, misunderstanding the situation we are in, and being confused about how reality works. Mistakes are breakdowns between the information "in here," in our minds, and the reality "out there," in the universe.

Mistakes are more likely when the situation is complicated or unfamiliar even when we are paying attention. But when we are pressured, hurried, careless, or confused, the subconscious mind may do the decision-making, and mistakes are much more likely.

Conversation about beliefs and babies

Let's go back to our student as she approaches her tutor with another question.

S. I've got another question about making mistakes. I understand that mistakes happen when the context I have in my mind doesn't match up with reality. Sometimes I don't understand something, and I use the wrong mental model. I get that, but shouldn't I learn from my mistake and pick a better model the next time? Why do people make the same mistake over and over? Don't they learn?

T. You're asking a really tough question, and the answer isn't always very flattering to our species. The truth is we sometimes are taught things and learn things that just aren't true. When we believe these falsehoods and act on them, we make mistakes.

S. Why would anyone teach me something that isn't true?

T. The innocent explanation is that the teacher may just be wrong. When teachers told their kids that the world was flat and the Earth was the center of the universe, they were just wrong. They didn't know better until learning caught up with the truth.

S. Okay. I get that; even teachers don't always know. I guess as science advances, teachers won't make this kind of mistake.

T. We can hope, but there is so much to know that even a good teacher has only so much knowledge. It's part of a teacher's job to be very sensitive to what those boundaries are.

S. You said this was an innocent explanation. Is there another kind?

T. Sadly, yes. Some people tell lies. Some people do it on purpose because they want us to believe things they have chosen and want us to act in ways that suit their purposes. These are demagogues. con men, and frauds They use their communication skills to plant lies in our minds and convince us to believe the lies. Such people take advantage of some of the limitations and features of our minds to gain money, power, or popularity for themselves. This is bad behavior.

S. You said, "some people do it on purpose." Is it possible that some people do this bad thing by accident?

T. Yes. That happens too. A teacher might believe a falsehood to be true and, without meaning harm, teach it to others. Not a lie, but still wrong. Spreading information, beliefs, or wrong mental models is one of the most dangerous things that minds do to each other.

S. Ouch! How are we supposed to know when what we are told is wrong? Doesn't that make it hard to know whom to trust?

T. Yes. We teachers have to be very careful about the things we teach, and you students have to be very thoughtful and skeptical of the things you are being taught. Some things are pretty straightforward. If I teach you how to compute the square root of a number, you can test the knowledge because you can easily check the arithmetic. If I teach you the organs of the body, you can get information about how reasonable my lesson was by comparing it to the dissection of a pig. Good teachers give you evidence to support the things they teach.

S. That's why we do laboratory experiments in science classes. Right?

T. Yes, exactly. But for a lot of things we teach, we ask you to believe without actually giving you much evidence because the evidence is complicated or not easy to experience directly. We assert truths like the distance to the moon, and we expect that you will trust us even though we can't easily measure it with you. We call on our "authority" as teachers.

S. You're making beliefs sound kind of "iffy."

T. I doubt you're too surprised that beliefs are iffy. You've already learned that the mind's understanding of the world "out there" is never perfect. So I'm sure you're not too surprised that we sometimes have beliefs, perceptions, or incorrect mental models.

S. Now that you put it that way, I guess I shouldn't be surprised, but it's a downer. But does my imperfect knowledge of reality explain all my mistakes? I mean, I should be able to fix my understanding once I realize it's wrong.

T. Yes, sometimes. But remember that bias is another wrinkle in our thinking that can contribute to very persistent mistakes.

S. You've convinced me that my mind has a less-than-perfect model of reality, so I have to be cautious and skeptical. Plus, now I'm positively afraid of confirmation bias. All that uncertainty is making me nervous. I'm not sure my superpower is all that super.

T. Cheer up! Having a superpower is a terrific thing, even if it isn't a perfect power. And, believe it or not, there is a plus side to making mistakes.

S. What can possibly be good about making mistakes?

T. Think about babies. We all start with almost no knowledge at all, and in a few years, we know how to walk, talk, and do a hundred things to get what we want, entertain ourselves, and get along with other humans. We have learned about hard things and soft things and living things and things that aren't. We have learned about loud. And stinky. And wet. We have learned about gravity. We have learned what is safe. Before the first day of pre-K, we have learned to be people.

S. Okay, we learn a lot, but what does that have to do with mistakes?

T. Everything. Think about it for a minute. Where did all that knowledge come from?

S. From parents, I guess.

T. True, interacting with our parents, observing them, and imitating them is an essential source of sensory input, and we store up a lot of memories. Anything else?

S. Ohhhh … now I get it. Trial and error! We try things, and we make mistakes. We learn about our immediate world by touching it, tasting it, and trying to break it. At least that's what my baby brother did.

T. Yes, from the very beginning, we gather an enormous amount of information about reality by bumping into it. Every mistake we make provides the raw material that we can use to build a better mental model of the world. When we see that surprised look on a baby's face, we know she just learned something.

Investigation is what we call the process of discovering the things in the "out-there world." And investigation leads us to answer questions like "what is this? What's it like, how did it come to be this way?" The answers are thought-bundles about things, processes, and cause-and-effect relationship models. We build beliefs out of mistakes. Like Michelangelo sculpting David, our mistakes are experiences that chip away the results that aren't reality until only a useful understanding is left.

This trial and error process is how we feel our way around the reality in which we live. We use our experience of mistakes to improve our understanding. When we're young, we do a lot of trying and revising, and, as we age, we gradually settle on a reasonably stable set of beliefs. We grow up with a vast number of built-in beliefs about reality that are stored in our subconscious and used as thinking shortcuts. We call this maturity.

S.   Okay, we've learned something about shortcuts. I know that the subconscious stores thinking-shortcuts so that we can speed up our actions when we need to. How do we know when the shortcut is a good idea?

T.   Okay, good question. Start by explaining to me what the word "shortcut" means.

S.   Shortcuts are our built-in standard operating procedures. We see the usual things, and we take the usual actions without any more thinking about it. Shortcuts are about habits … habits of thought.

T.   Right, If we had to think through each usual situation consciously, we would be practically paralyzed. Anyone who has learned a physical skill like piano-playing or swinging a golf club has felt the change when we stop thinking about what to do, and the action just happens. Our subconscious grooves a pattern and makes it a shortcut for the mind.

S.   But there's some sort of problem?

T.   Yes, shortcuts are indispensable, but there's a downside. Reality is so complicated that no shortcut is going to fit every circumstance. The more involved and variable the situation, the less likely a thought habit will serve us well. The world in which our short-cut ability evolved was a lot less complicated than the world we confront today. Habits and other "thought-less" actions are more dangerous now than they were in the evolutionary past.

S. Are some shortcuts safer than others?

T. Sure. The place where our shortcut capability is most likely to be useful and least likely to be mistaken, is a physical habit – piano-playing, typing, etc. The place where the shortcut ability is most likely to get us in trouble is when the subconscious uses it to substitute for complex thinking. When situations are complex, the subconscious can hand off incorrect beliefs and warped perceptions to the Comparer and the Projector, leading us to critical errors.

S. My dad told me that when I come to a conclusion very fast, I should be extra cautious. I guess he meant I should make sure it wasn't a shortcut or a bias that was affecting my thinking.

T. Good advice. Your dad's pretty smart.

෧ ෧ ෧ ෨ ෨ ෨

We realize that a better understanding of reality leads to better thinking. But where does a better understanding come from? The answer, of course, is education. The next chapter is another example of talking about thinking. Specifically, Sandy and her tutor talk about the connection between education, good thinking, and good results.

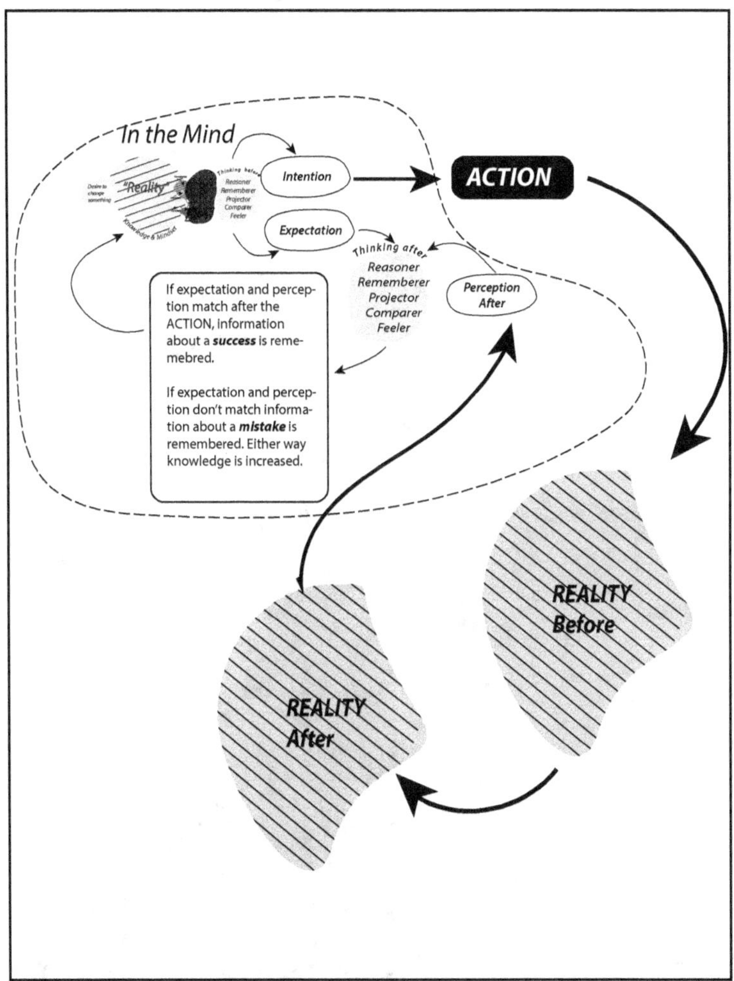

There is a feedback loop – desire, decision, intent and expectation, action, perception, comparison of new perceived reality with expectation — we use to adjust "Reality" in the mind. That's "learning from experience."

Based on image by Museums Victoria

Chapter 12
Talking About Education

HERE WE TAKE another chapter to see how the 21st-Century Mind model boosts our ability to talk about thinking. But before Sandy and her tutor engage in another conversation, there are things to mention first.

Thinking about thinking

Despite being complicated and error-prone, conscious thinking is a vital part of our human superpower. But conscious thinking is a fragile process. If we want to use our superpower to best advantage, we need to pay attention to how our minds work and apply what we learn.

As children, we never thought about thinking. We just did it. That's what many of us do our whole lives. We use our minds, but we don't give any attention to how we use them. Our minds just do what minds do, and our lives just happen.

For most of us, no one explicitly told us anything about the structure of our minds or how our minds relate to our brains. No one cautioned us about the limitations of our perceptions. No one said anything about how reliable our memories are or how our feelings affect our decision-making. Our minds "just growed."

Here's a thought experiment. Imagine a child, middle-school age, but ignorant of airplanes. Call him Orville. Put Orville in a plane's empty cockpit while it's flying. What happens?

Orville eventually begins to investigate … turn the yoke, move the throttle handles, and push buttons more or less at random. If he's lucky, he will learn how to steer left and right, up and down without crashing the plane. Luckier still, he may learn how to make the plane speed up or slow down. He may find out how to lower the landing gear. Imagine now, Orville manages to make a landing and survives. Would we say that he was a good pilot? Hardly.

The plane with the child in the cockpit is the analog of what we get if a healthy person has a fully-functioning brain and a mind that develops at random.

Of course, we don't usually let that happen. Orville learns from parents, peers, and educators. He develops a mindset with beliefs, values, and principles. He conceives, refines, and stores mental models, memories, and cause-and-effect relationships. He builds a mind. Even with very rudimentary teaching, human children raised by humans, become people. We let the kids interact with reality, watch us use our minds, and then expect they will figure out how to use theirs. A mind is gathered, but rarely examined.

We've spent the previous chapters examining minds. We imagined a hierarchy of beliefs, values, principles. We focused on mental models as the stuff on which the thought process acts. We imagined the various tools like Rememberer, Projector, and Reasoner that the mind uses. We've got a mental model complete with the names of the major parts and a high-level description of how they work. We know the 21ˢᵗ-Century Mind model.

Are we done? Is the 21ˢᵗ-Century Mind model all a kid needs to know? Of course not. Just as Orville, the young flyer, might be given a useful description of the parts of a plane and he might be prepared to take flying lessons … he isn't a pilot. Having a useful description of a mind by itself, does not make a thinker. Running our mind's decision-factory is like flying, juggling, or playing the bassoon; we learn to do it by doing, reviewing, and improving. To become a pilot (or a thinker), Orville needs an appropriate education.

Conversation about education and thinking

T. Would you like an extra credit assignment on a new topic for the weekend?

S. Sure, I like new stuff, and I don't have any grand plans.

T. Good. Here's the assignment. Bring in at least five quotations from educators that talk about why education is essential. Okay?

S. Sure. I can do that. Do you want to tell me why?

T. Education has been a goal for all of recorded history. We have at least 5000 years of experimentation, experience, and evaluation of techniques and tools for teaching. Why is it so important? How does the study we've been doing about the mind fit in with the broader goals of education? That's what we'll be talking about next.

S. Okay. I got it. See you Monday.

Here are paraphrases* our student collected from the writings of some deep thinkers about education. Speaking of education, they said, education:

- Creates men and women who can do new things, not merely repeat what others have done.
- Teaches one to think intensively and critically.
- Enables entertaining a thought without accepting it.
- Empowers clear thinking.
- Replaces an empty mind with an open one.
- Passes society's soul from one generation to another.
- Moves from darkness to light.
- Teaches what you didn't even know you didn't know.
- Prepares the young to educate themselves.
- Is the very spring and root of honesty and virtue.
- Disciplines, but does not over-stuff the mind.
- Educates hearts as well as minds

After reviewing the list, the dialog between teacher and student resumes.

---

*Quotes paraphrased from Marilyn Price-Mitchell Ph.D. (Price-Mitchell 2014)

T. (smiling broadly) So, I asked for five quotes, and you brought me 12. You must have liked this assignment.

S. I did. You know we spend so much time on education, and I never gave much thought to why. I mean, kids have to go to school and we mostly just do it 'cause we're supposed to. I never really thought about why it's important.

T. Surely your parents have had something to say on that subject.

S. Yes. They say stuff like, "Your education is the most important thing you have, and nobody can take it away." Stuff like that. Older kids say that I should get an education so I can get a better job and make a lot of money. That's okay, but it doesn't sound much like what all those quotes were talking about.

T. (nodding) It's pretty clear that most of the cultures our species has developed have thought highly of education. Especially in the last few hundred years. Our education efforts absorb an enormous amount of our society's time, energy, and resources. I'm going to mention some of the subjects that we teach in school. See if you can tell me why they are important. Use the ideas from the mind model. Can you do that?

S. I'll try.

T. Good. Let's start with the simplest things. Why do we teach children language and reading?

S. Well, I guess we teach kids to talk 'cause we want to talk to them. That's how older people pass on thought-bundles about the world.

T. Most kids can talk before they start school, but you're right. Education starts from baby's first conversation with Mom, way before the kid gets to school. What about reading?

S. I guess we have to read before we can learn all the things that are in books.

T. Yes, in teacher-talk, "We teach language and reading so that we can open the doors of human knowledge." What kind of human knowledge do you think we're talking about?

S. (eagerly) Thought-bundles! Lots of bundles about things like ducks and planets and lots of bundles about cause-and-effect like long division or how we make laws. Lots of bundles!

T. Yes, indeed. We teach facts – math, science, history – so that young minds will have useful mental models to build on. If we do it right, our graduates have a lot of useful beliefs about reality. That's about facts. Why do you suppose we teach literature, lots of the facts in stories are fiction, not real.

S. I'm kind of stumped on that one. Why do we need to read fiction if it isn't real?

T. We teach literature and art so that students will know human behavior beyond their direct experience. You've never floated down the Mississippi, but you've read Huckleberry Finn, so you know something about the time and place of the story and the behavior of slaves like Jim or con-men like the Duke. You also learned something about American culture in Mark Twain's time.

S. I guess that's right, but I certainly didn't think about it then. It was just a story. But I guess I got the thought-bundles even though I didn't notice. So that's education; filling up our minds with thought-bundles?

T. That, yes, but it turns out there is a lot more to it. We fill young minds with thought-bundles, then we encourage them to practice thinking. That's the tricky part for teachers and often the hard part for students. We ask you, students, to practice, drill, and rehearse the facts and to train your minds to think … to investigate, to evaluate, to project, and to innovate. We ask you to practice with the parts of knowledge, to practice with the processes of assembling the pieces into a whole, and then we say, rehearse, review, and polish your performance. We ask you to practice thinking so that healthy thinking becomes a habit.

S. So, education is really about thinking and learning to use our minds?

T. Exactly!

S. Why doesn't anybody say so?

The student's question is the question that we all should be asking. Education is dedicated, heart and soul, to teaching our children to think, but **we avoid saying so**. Such neglect must change.

Teaching a suitable mental model of mind will amplify, not dilute, education. The suitable mental model of mind is a lynch-pin that we can insert into our education system with very little disturbance but huge benefit.

It would be pathology and educational malpractice to teach dancing without mentioning feet, legs, or balance; to teach sailing without mentioning boats, rudders, or sails; or to teach driving without saying brakes, wheels, or steering. How can we effectively teach thinking if we don't mention the mind, if we don't name its functions, and we fail to point out its strengths, weaknesses, or quirks? It's time we give our children a foundational learning-standard and an appropriate learning progression in the mind's subject matter. Let's tell them as often as we can that we are teaching them to use their minds.

In this chapter and the last, we have eavesdropped on Sandy and her tutor using the vocabulary of the 21ˢᵗ-Century Mind model as they have talked about making mistakes and then as they talked about the relationship of education to thinking. In the next chapter, Sandy gets another assignment from her tutor and they have a conversation about where most of us get our thoughts about minds.

Takeaway — Thinking and education

- A useful model of mind is necessary but not sufficient to make a good thinker.

- Successful thinking requires a well-equipped mind – useful knowledge, mental models, and beliefs – and practice using it.

- We call the work of building and exercising a well-equipped mind "education."

- We teach language and reading to open the doors to human knowledge.

- Education fills memory with useful thought-bundles: facts, mental process-models, cause-and-effect relations, and descriptions of human behavior.

- When we study, we store and connect these thought-bundles, then we practice with them in novel situations.

Based on images by Sarad Shrestha and Cliff Johnson

Chapter 13
Talking About Folk Wisdom

IN THE LAST CHAPTER, high-school age Sandy and her tutor talked about the value of education and observed that children are rarely taught about thinking. In this chapter, they continue their conversation and dig into what people do to try to improve their thinking in spite of that sad fact.

Conversation about the folk wisdom of better decisions

T. Ready for another extra-credit assignment?

S. Sure, why not. The last one was sort of fun.

T. This one is pretty simple. I want you to collect some examples of folk wisdom about better thinking. By folk wisdom, I mean the sorts of things that popular writers and self-help gurus suggest when we want to improve some thinking task.

S. Okay. What should I google?

T. Here are two topics: "How to improve decision making" and "How to be more creative." See if you can find lists of suggestions and pick out a few of the most popular ones. Bring them in, and we'll talk about them. Got it?

S. Got it.

Now, our student, with her assignment about folk wisdom, is back. She has searched the internet for suggestions about how to improve thinking and their conversation resumes.

S. Well, here it is. I selected twenty documents from the search, "Making better decisions." I sorted and summarized the lists. I know this was the assignment, but this was really unscientific. There were lots of duplicates. It seems that one writer is likely to copy from the others.

T. That's okay. You might say this approach reflects the haphazard, informal, pop-culture way most people get their information about decision-making. Did you find anything unusual about the suggestions?

S. Yes, it struck me that all the popular tips about making better decisions are concerned with conscious choices. There didn't seem to be anything about all the decisions our subconscious makes.

T. That's not surprising, is it? As a culture, we don't seem to acknowledge that decisions "without thinking" are really decisions. What were the suggestions like?

S. There were two kinds of suggestions. There were the "how-tos" … things like "set criteria, use data," or "brainstorm options."

T. Yes, those were practical additions to the mental process models.

S. Yeah, and then there were twice as many suggestions that advised on the frame of mind we should have when we are making decisions … things like "get an outside perspective, involve other people, get outside your information bubble."

T. How would you characterize these suggestions in terms of our model of mind?

S. Hmmm. Are these intended to help us deal with bias? I mean, other people with a different mindset probably don't have the same biases.

T. I think that's it exactly. Is there anything you can say about all the suggestions about decision making?

S. Nearly all of this advice focuses on things to assure that I get my mindset right and use the right mental model of the situation.

T. Exactly. The how-to advice is intended to get an appropriate amount of information into our belief set. The other suggestions try to make sure that a conscious decision not be slanted, preempted, or corrupted by the subconscious mind. But you still didn't find much discussion of the role of the subconscious, right?

S.   No, the word didn't come up in the lists I found on-line.

T.   Not a surprise. The received wisdom of our age includes an understanding of the critical role the subconscious plays in the way we make our choices … but most often we don't talk about it.

Conversation about the folk wisdom of creativity

T.   What about the other part of the assignment?

S.   Yes, the second part, about creativity, was a lot more interesting. The search was "How to be more creative." It was more interesting because the suggestions were all over the place and some of them were weird. I kind of dug into the creativity suggestions.

T.   How did you "dig in?"

S.   I looked at 15 lists that gave me 189 different suggestions to make us more creative. There were general themes about creating something by having a better or richer mental model. They suggested stretching the model with approaches like changing the names of things or trying to imagine your work as a sport. They suggested enriching your mental model by imagining trying to achieve the exact opposite of your goal, reading something weird, or talking to children or older people. Some suggestions seemed to be attempts to call on the subconscious like daydreaming, practicing mindfulness, or taking a nap.

T.   Did they mention mental models or the subconscious?

S.   No, but that's what they were really talking about.

Shortcomings of folk wisdom

We often suffer from the consequences of insufficient, inappropriate, or just plain wrong-headed thinking. Some of us take our suffering to a shrink; we treat our poor thinking as a disease. However, most of us never get to the shrink's office, and we rarely, if ever, are exposed to any formal model of mind … even an unsuitable, useless one. How bad is this situation? This bad … most of us have a better mental model of our cars than of our minds!

Really, cars!

Even preschoolers can tell us what a car is, but ask most adults what a mind is then stand back for a lot of mumbling, stumbling, and head-scratching. We use the word "mind," but we have only the foggiest idea what it refers to.

Even very young children know what a car does and what we use it for: "we go to the store, to school, and to Grandma's house.," but few of us could give a concise and coherent explanation of what we use our minds for.

Most people can list the functions of a car … starting, going forward and backward, stopping, and turning. We all know about major car parts … engines, wheels, tires, etc. How many of us would be able to make a similar list of significant functions and components of minds?

Such ignorance should embarrass us. Thinking is our superpower. Studying it should be part of every human's education. Children should be taught about this gift, but sadly they're not.

It's not that we aren't interested in better thinking. We most definitely are. In the absence of proper training, we resort to what little is available. We binge on folk wisdom.

It's clear by now that any discussion of how to do better thinking requires a mental model of the mind, but the models aren't there. Writers and speakers don't talk about what lies beneath their suggestions, recommendations, and nostrums. They talk about "how to" but don't explain "why."

With nothing but folk wisdom to rely on, our actions are hobbled by failure to understand several key things. Folk wisdom doesn't explain that our perceptions are limited. It doesn't expose the central importance of mental models to understanding reality, and it doesn't help us understand the fragility and malleability of memory or the complex interplay of emotion with perception, memory, and anticipation.

Folk wisdom fails to explain how we understand the past or anticipate the future. Folk wisdom only hints at the profound influence beliefs, values, and principles have on our actions.

Folk wisdom often seems to ignore the massive role of the subconscious and the ebb and flow of consciousness. We are given nothing about the interplay of awareness and attention. We all know, without thinking too deeply about it, that folk wisdom isn't sufficient to guide vital thinking tasks. We shouldn't despise this folk wisdom; it has its place. Neither should we trust folk wisdom when it truly matters.

∾ ∾ ∾ ∿ ∿ ∿

We conclude that folk wisdom is a weak crutch for critical thinking. Still, in some situations, our society has slowly developed expectations, customs, and laws that seek to ensure good thinking despite the mind's limitations. In the next chapter, we listen in while Sandy and her tutor talk about three examples where our culture seeks to protect us from poor thinking.

Image by John Salvino

Chapter 14
Talking About Safeguards

SOME GROUP THINKING TASKS are particularly important to living successfully together and making progress as a species. Our cultures have assembled customs, laws, processes, and rules to govern critical tasks. In this chapter, we listen to Sandy and her tutor talking about how, in special situations, these cultural adaptations try to buttress our thinking against the mind's limitations.

Our student is about to examine three critical examples concerned with investigation and understanding. She has a question.

S. Do you remember when you told us that our evolution has left us with some features of our minds that are good for the human species but sometimes aren't so good for us as individuals?

T. Sure, we mentioned that when we were learning about the way inclinations and conceptual balances are distributed. Also, when we talked about the role of feelings. But most importantly, I guess when we dug into the role that the subconscious sometimes plays if we react without involving the Reasoner.

S. Yes, all of that. We learned that humans didn't get the way we are to make us happy. We are the way we are because that was how we survived. I get that, and you've taught us that the best way to guard against obsolete knee jerk actions is to think before we act. My question is a little complicated.

T. Go on.

S. Okay. I think humans have been doing more conscious thinking as we've gone along. I mean, we're probably not smarter than the cave people, but to just cope with the changes we've made ourselves, we've had to learn more stuff and think about things more. To me, it looks like the progression from the stone age to today has required a lot of cultural change that takes us beyond simple evolution. Is that right?

T. Sure, once we got the superpower, we started learning how to use it, and we still are. That's social evolution.

S. Well, what I want to know is, does this social evolution involve some understanding of the limitations of the superpower? I mean, as a group, have we figured out how to use the superpower and avoid the mistakes we can still make?

T. I suspect that the answer to your question is, "We're beginning to figure it out." Let's dig into some social activities where I think we've made some progress. Let's talk about three different kinds of investigation. Do you remember how we described investigation in the model?

S. Investigation means that we are using our minds to answer the question, "How did things get to be the way they are?" We also learned that the question, "What will happen if …?" is almost the same as far as the mind is concerned. Investigation of both questions requires the best mental model of the situation we can get, especially cause-and-effect models.

T. Okay, you nailed it!

Conversation about journalism

T. Let's start by taking a look at journalism … you know, the business of gathering the news and distributing it. What's the difference between good journalism and bad journalism? Can you think of three things?

S. Well, I can only think of one. Good journalism has to be true. What else matters?

T. I agree that truth, accuracy, and strict adherence to facts is centrally important, but I also think that the reporting has to be timely — who cares about yesterday's news? Also, it has to be understandable — presentation matters. Agreed?

S. Yes. True, timely, and clear. If it's true, but it isn't timely, that's history. If it's true and timely, but it isn't understandable, it probably isn't very useful. Timely and understandable sounds like good journalism, but I still think truth is most important.

T. Okay. Agreed. Now go do a little research and tell me what we mean by "journalistic ethics."

While our student is researching, let's take a moment to note how remarkable it is that we have developed journalism as a profession and that within the profession, there are such things as journalistic ethics. In recent history, our idea of the "news" has evolved from neighborhood gossip, to town crier, to broadsheets and newspapers, and then to the radio, newsreels, and "the TV evening news." Now we have all of these plus a complex of news channels, internet-based social media, and news consolidators. Technology has taken the mind's power to share information and exploded it into a mosaic of sources, not all of which ever adopted anything like journalistic ethics.

S. I'm back. I found the main goals of journalistic ethics, as stated in their professional guide (Society of Professional Journalists 2014). First, "Seek truth and report it." I guess putting truth first is how the profession emphasizes the importance of fact thought-bundles and the underlying cause-and-effect models they report on. After that, the guide says, "Minimize Harm," "Act Independently", and "Be Accountable and Transparent."

T. What do you think, "Be accountable and transparent means?"

S. I think it's their way of saying, "If you have a bias, tell what it is."

T. Do you think that the statement of professional ethics exerts much influence on the news we're exposed to?

S. There are lots of details in the code of ethics. Following each goal statement, there are several statements that the 21st-Century Mind model calls principles. The ethics code as a whole seems to be a particular mindset designed for people who are acting as journalists. But I think there's a problem.

T. Tell me.

S. Yeah, there are certainly journalists who are very careful about the ethical goals and the principles that support them, but there is just so much stuff out there that seems to be news, and I never know

> where most of it comes from. I doubt everybody who writes or talks about "news" is ethical about it. I don't know who to believe or what to trust.
>
> T   I agree. Modern communication is so fast, even the most ethical reporter is likely to get the facts and the underlying story wrong sometimes. And the not-so-ethical reporters have a million ways to get it wrong through carelessness, prejudice, or malice.
>
> S.   (shrugging) It's kind of creepy, isn't it?. Society hasn't done such a good job preventing thinking mistakes in the news.
>
> T.   Let's give ourselves some credit for trying. When you think about it, it's a relatively new problem. I suspect we'll keep trying to sort it out because it's essential, especially in a democracy, to get as good a grasp on reality as we can.

News media transfers information from sender-mind to receiver-mind to add to or alter, for better or worse, the mindset, thought-bundles, and mental models of the receiver. Because reporting is a human activity, unbiased reporting is an ideal, but never a reality. When media sources slant information to fit an opinion, their biases may be intentional or subconscious. When media intentionally distorts facts and employs specific techniques to force a desired position on their consumers, reporting becomes propaganda.

The conscious mind is the only protection we have from propaganda. News is a tsunami, often polluted by opinion and bias. Only frequent conscious and fearless self-examination is protection from these waves. For us, as individuals, the examined mind becomes more and more critical. This, of course, isn't new, just more urgent as our communication technology has advanced. Our society leaves it to our individual minds to sort ethical journalism from everything else that washes over us.

Conversation about criminal law

Reliance on individual minds isn't safe enough for some critical purposes. The teacher is about to ask our student to tackle another area where getting it right is even more urgent.

> T. You had useful insights into the way journalism tries to cope with the limitations of mind. I'd like you to try a similar examination of another area. Okay?
>
> S. Okay. Is this one harder?
>
> T. Yes, harder, but I think, clearer. I'd like us to have a conversation about how our society deals with the limitations of mind in the area of criminal law. Do some research. Just focus on the U.S., okay?

In the last few centuries, developed cultures have invented a complex web of rules and constraints about how we should deal with the problems of crime. Most of us would agree that our current system isn't perfect. It's enormously complicated and expensive, but we'd also agree that criminal law and procedure are much fairer and more humane than they were in the past. Let's see what our student has to say about how criminal law deals with the limitations of mind.

> S. I focused on four roles: what police do, what prosecutors do, what juries do, and what judges do. I didn't get into much detail because I thought it was concepts we should talk about …why the roles were conceived as they have been.
>
> T. Good. Let's hear it.
>
> S. When a crime is committed, we expect the police to identify the criminal. Police collect and document what they believe to be useful information about the crime and the suspected criminal. They investigate. They are the first people to officially propose an explanation of how the crime was committed and who did it. They write down the thought-bundles of facts and the cause-and-effect model of what happened.
>
> T. You make it sound very formal.
>
> S. Well, I guess it's supposed to be. People who do this job often complain about all the bureaucracy and paperwork. I think it works that way in the hope that subjectivity gets squeezed out of the information. I don't know if it does, but I think that's the theory.
>
> T. Okay. What comes next?
>
> S. The next role is the prosecutor. The prosecutor's job starts by seeing how the police information matches up with the law and whether or not the information is complete enough to bring a

charge against the person the police think is a criminal. If it is, the processes of the court against the alleged criminal begin.

T. How would you describe the prosecutor's thinking?

S. She thinks about the police mental model of the crime with all the available thought-bundles. She decides if there is a good chance that she can persuade others that the information is probably a good representation of reality. It's supposed to be a high hurdle – "beyond a reasonable doubt."

T. So, if she thinks it's a good case, she can take it to a trial. Then there will be a defense lawyer, witnesses, and your other two roles … judge and jury, right? How do their rules deal with the limitations of the mind?

S. The purpose of the trial is to get at the truth. I guess that means to get a mental model of what happened that is as close to reality as possible. The judge decides what fact-bundles can be introduced into the situation and what the opposing lawyers can say to affect the belief-set the jurors end up with. The trial is all about shaping a mental model in the minds of the people in the jury. The judge tries to keep it fair by controlling the thought-bundles and the way the lawyers try propaganda tricks to influence the jurors' mindsets.

T. Is that it? The lawyers shape a mindset for the jury, and the judge tries to keep it fair?

S. There's one more crucial part. The jury has to agree on what happened. That means they talk about the case until, as a group, they settle on a mental model of what happened and whether or not the fact bundles are sufficient to remove any reasonable doubt. A jury is a big group, usually twelve people, and I guess the idea is that the mindsets and biases that the jurors start with kind of cancel out and somehow just leave the information from the trial.

T. You sound a little skeptical.

S. Well, I understand the purpose, and there are a lot of rules about how this all works, and the opposing lawyers are supposed to balance out, but it seems like there are still a lot of ways our minds can be fooled and fool us. After all, juries are just "us."

T. Your skepticism is healthy, but I guess we need to remember that this process, too, is relatively new, and we may get better at it as we go along. The important thing to remember is that our society has begun working out how to deal with the shortcomings and limitations of our minds, even though we rarely talk about it that way.

Criminal law is a thinking discipline. Thinking disciplines have evolved to confront the fact that a human mind can never construct a mental model as complex as the reality it represents and that the mindset's beliefs, principles, and biases are an inevitable part of being human. Criminal law is designed to accommodate the quirks and limitations of human minds in the investigation of crime and punishment. Its application is a particularly sensitive process that requires careful thinking, carefully constrained. Ponderous and awkward at times, criminal law codifies our society's efforts to offset the limitations of mind.

There is another, even more important, thinking discipline that our student will take up next.

Conversation about science

T. You've done good work. You've told me about journalism. You explained that professional ethics are an attempt to keep the appearance and essence of reporting close to reality. Then you told me about how the roles in the criminal justice system are designed to avoid mistakes and bias. There's one more kind of investigation I'd like you to think about. Okay?

S. Is it as complicated as the criminal justice thing? That was hard.

T. You can answer that question yourself when you're done. This time I want you to examine the way our society has organized scientific investigation to counter the frailties of the human mind. Can you do that?

S. I'm not much of a science person, and it sounds pretty hard, but I'll try.

The teacher asks our student to briefly describe the value of science – why do we do it? And then to explain how scientists try to make sure that the mind's limitations don't compromise their work. Here's what she reported.

S. The first question was, "Why do we need science?" It got me thinking about what science is and why it's important. I never thought about it before, but now I believe that there isn't much else that people do more important than science.

T.   That's a bold statement. Please explain.

S.   Anthropology and history tell us that people have been gradually accumulating information for a very long time, thousands of years from fire and the wheel to space flight and DNA. It's hard to separate science from invention and engineering, but all technology depends ultimately on science. Science is our shared library of fact thought-bundles and mental models that describe how reality works. Science is especially important when we are trying to understand the reality that we can't directly perceive. And, as we learned, we can't directly perceive most of it.

T.   Example, please.

S.   Hmmm … how's this? We can't get any useful personal information about precisely what fire is even if we get burned. It's the science that explains why stuff like wood combines with oxygen to give off heat. Or another example, we needed the work of scientists before we could understand why things fall down instead of up or why the moon doesn't fall down at all.

T.   Good examples. So I hear you saying that science is a collection of knowledge that people we call scientists have gathered and written down to explain things about reality that aren't obvious to us. That our simple perceptions tend to lead to mistakes and science gives us a better basis for thinking about some situations. Is that it?

S.   Well, yes, but that's a lot of words. I'd maybe just say science can make us less ignorant so we can act less stupid.

T.   (laughs) Good one! Now tell me why we trust astronomy not astrology, psychology not phrenology, or chemistry not alchemy. That was the second part of the assignment.

S.   You taught us that beliefs are assertions about reality that we trust enough to act on. We trust science because scientists try to be very clear about the mental models they use and careful about separating their opinions and biases from the statements they make about reality. It's their clarity and carefulness that gives us a reason to trust what they say. And that's the difference between real science and pseudoscience — special clarity and carefulness.

T. How is this special carefulness expressed? What do scientists do that makes their assertions more trustworthy than others?

S. I guess I should start by saying that just being a scientist doesn't make a person's general opinions more trustworthy than anybody else's. That's because scientists have specialties. A scientist in chemistry can make assertions about molecules and how they behave that non-experts are likely to trust, but the same scientist is just another fan when it comes to which baseball team is best.

T. Good explanation, scientists are experts in some area of science. How do they get that way?

S. They go to school. A lot! And in schools they study the thought-bundles, especially cause-and-effect models, that generations of scientists have accumulated.

T. Is that it? Scientists just learn what previous scientists already have figured out?

S. No! It's much better than that. Yes, new scientists are supposed to learn what's already known about their subjects. But they are also supposed to learn a meticulous process mental model about how to add to the total knowledge. It's called "the scientific method." It's the scientific method where the safeguards are built in about the limitations of the mind.

T. Can you give an example?

S. Sure. The method starts with some mental model of whatever the scientist is researching. The researcher says, "if my model is correct, then, when I do this experiment, I will observe this predicted result. If I don't get the predicted outcome, then the model was probably wrong.

T. Is that it? Scientists do experiments?

S. No, there's a lot more to it. It's especially important to science as a whole for each scientist to publish the results of their experiments. Other experts look very carefully at the published details of the experiments and results. They check for mistakes and biases. They argue about the possible meanings of the experiments, and they push each other to do more thinking, experimenting, and publishing.

T. How would you summarize science in terms of our model of the mind?

> S. Hmmmmm … let's see. Science is a collection of fact-bundles, process models, and cause-and-effect models about the nature of reality. The collection is written down by experts who have agreed to test and carefully expand the collection's facts and models.
>
> T. Excellent work! Maybe you should think of yourself as a science person after all.

In the last four chapters, teacher and student examined how and why we make mistakes, talked about the mind as an essential part of education, reviewed the shortcomings of folk wisdom, and discussed what our society has done to recognize and protect against some human thinking weaknesses. Conversations like these strengthen our young people and our entire society.

If we can talk coherently about thinking, we can explain to our children the strengths and weaknesses of their superpower. A suitable model of mind is indispensable to that conversation. There should be no doubt that we can adopt a suitable mental model of mind, learn it, and teach it to our children. It's simple, inexpensive, and straightforward. The next section of the book gives some guidance on how to do it.

Takeaway — Safeguards

- Customs, laws, and rules have evolved in some critical areas of human culture to protect societies from the limitations of the human mind.

- Journalism, criminal law, and science are three of these areas.

- Even though the areas are critical, the protections are far from perfect.

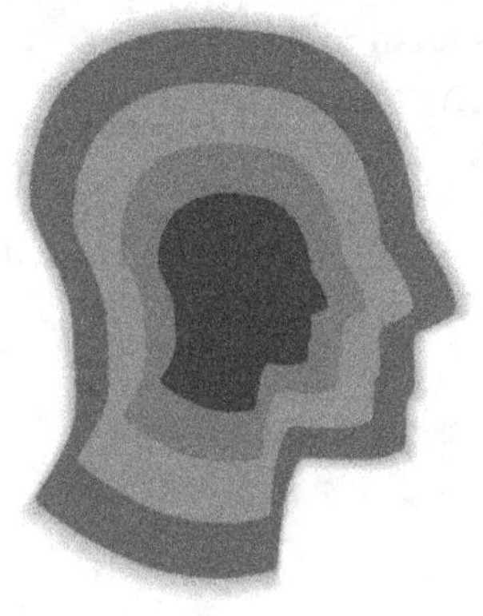

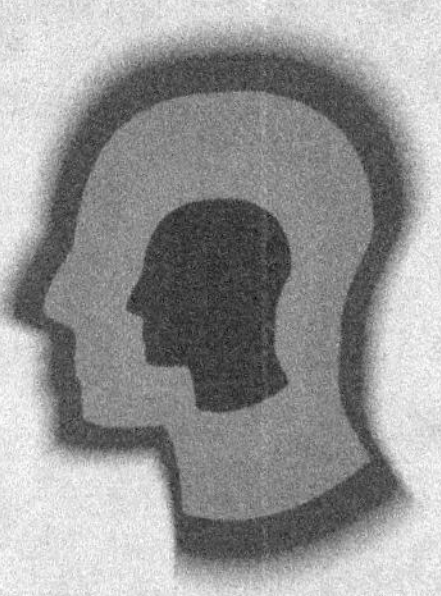

TEACHING A SUITABLE MODEL OF MIND

Based on images by Sarad Shrestha and Element5 Digital

Chapter 15
Teaching and Learning

AUSEFUL MIND MODEL BENEFITS each of us. We make better personal decisions, fewer mistakes. Benefits extend to everyone when a lot of us share a useful mental model of mind. We're all better off when we teach this stuff to our kids, and they don't have to wait for college to begin learning it; they can start in preschool.

This chapter outlines a course of study to illustrate the possible pedagogic progression and material that will be adopted as students become more experienced with the vocabulary and concepts of the 21st-Century Mind.

Preschool and elementary school

Children understand abstract concepts beginning as young as four years (Bransford 2000). At that age, a lecture hall approach is clearly inappropriate. Certainly, though, the literature is full of techniques to interest and introduce preschoolers to science abstractions like energy, growth, and friction, and social abstractions like freedom, temptation, and kindness. Good teachers use concrete items, active play, and questions to build bridges from the child's existing knowledge to these new ideas.

Recall in Chapter 1 there was a dialog between our tutor and Bobby, a five-year-old who likes to play with stickers. You may want to reread it. Young Bobby learned, "My mind is the part of me that makes me me." When repeated often enough, this thought puts the idea of mind front-and-center in his concept of self.

Mental models are almost as fundamental as the concept of mind itself. That earlier conversation with Bobby also added the idea of a model as a representation of toys to an understanding already present in the mind. In addition, the notion of model illustrated the difference between real and imagined things — a concept even young children understand. Finally, the conversation established the idea that models are entirely in the mind until they are shared. Youngsters get this idea too.

Individual kids develop at different rates and find materials about minds and thinking differently appealing. Still, most grade-school kids are comfortable with the basics of the 21st-Century Mind model. The following few sections have additional dialogs taking place when Bobby is in first grade.

Conversation about the functions of memory

Memory is so central to the idea of mind and thinking that it pays to get the idea started with children as soon as possible. This conversation with Bobby, now seven, continues the dialogs from Chapter 1.

T. Do you remember what we learned about which part of you makes you you?

S. (distractedly) Uh-huh, my mind makes me me.

T. Exactly! Your mind has to do a lot of things to make a person as special as you. Would you like to find out what some of those things are?

S. (looking up) Maybe. Is it fun?

T. I hope so; let's start with a question. What did you have for breakfast?

S. Mom gave me cereal and orange juice.

T. Good, how do you know that?

S, I remembered it.

T. That's right, you have a memory of cereal and juice. Where is that memory; where do you keep it? In your toe? In your elbow? Where is the memory?

S. (Looks at tutor skeptically, then …) Oh, I know! The cereal and juice are in my mind!

T. Exactly right! Your mind makes up memories and saves them.

S. (with a mischievous smile) You mean like pockets?

T. Not exactly like pockets, but your mind does have a special place in your brain to save memories, your mind pays attention to the things you do and see and keeps the important ones in your memory. You know what else?

S. What?

T. Your mind also reaches into that special place and takes out your memory so you can answer the question about breakfast. That's four things your mind does for you. It pays attention, it makes memories, it saves the memories, and it gets them back when you need them. Pretty special, Eh? Do you want to know some more?

S. (dubiously) Okay, I guess.

T. Here's another question. What are you going to have for lunch?

S. I'm not sure. Mom probably will give me a sandwich and milk.

T. Did you remember the sandwich and milk?

S. Well, no. They haven't happened yet.

T. Okay, your thought about lunch isn't exactly a memory because it hasn't happened yet. I imagine that you have memories of other lunches that helped you guess about today, right?

S. Uh-huh, Mom always gives me a sandwich … unless we have pizza.

T. So, you remembered other lunches and imagined lunch today. Imagining is a lot like remembering except for things that haven't happened yet. What part of you does the remembering?

S. (impatient) My mind.

T. Right, so what part do you think does the imagining?

S. (more impatient) My mind!

T. Yes, exactly. That's another thing your mind does. It builds thoughts that are a lot like memories, except they haven't happened yet. We

> call these kinds of thoughts, expectations, or forecasts. Or guesses, or just imaginings. More things that your mind does. Make sense?
>
> S. I guess. Are we done?
>
> T. Yes. It's time for lunch.

This conversation introduces the ideas of memories as things that are available in the mind and that the mind stores and recalls. The point is made that memories and projections are very similar and that both are manipulated by the mind.

Conversation about comparison as a mind function

This next dialog with Bobby introduces the idea of comparing things and leads directly to the concept of using a mind to make decisions.

> T. Is your mind functioning this morning?
>
> S. (reluctantly), I guess. Maybe.
>
> T. Do you remember when we talked about the things a mind does?
>
> S. Yeah, we talked about it last time — remembering. My mind does that for me.
>
> T. Anything else?
>
> S. (looking away) I can't remember.
>
> T. What do you think we'll talk about today?
>
> S. (exasperation) More stuff about minds?
>
> T. How did you figure that out?
>
> S. (confusion, then surprise) Ohhhhh … my mind helps me imagine and expect things too.
>
> T. Very good. Our minds have a Rememberer part and a Projector part. The Remember part saves memories of things that we see happen, and the Projector part lets us imagine what could happen.
>
> S. (tiredly) Does my mind have to do anything else?
>
> T. How about this: which is better, a cookie or a paper clip?
>
> S. A cookie, of course.
>
> T. Which is better: one cookie or two cookies?
>
> S. Two cookies!

T. Which is better: a chocolate chip cookie or an oatmeal cookie?

S. (frowning) That's hard. I like them both.

T. Okay. I understand. Let's change that: which is better one chocolate chip or two oatmeal?

S. (brightens) Easy, two oatmeal.

T. Yup, so here's what you said to me: a cookie is better than a paper clip, two cookies are better than one cookie, and even though chocolate chip and oatmeal cookies are pretty much equally desirable, two oatmeal are better than one chocolate chip. You've decided a lot of things in the last minute or two. How did you do it?

S. (pleased) Ohhhh … I got it. My mind helped me decide.

T. Exactly! You're catching on. Let's review what you did. You compared things. Your mind has a Comparer that lets you know when things are different sizes or different importance, and it tells you when things are the same. That's pretty useful, isn't it, when you have to decide to get a cookie or paper clip.

S. (smiles) Cookies are better. I can't eat a paper clip.

T. Next question. Imagine that you have a pile of papers, you straighten them up, and now that they are neat, you want to keep them that way. Do you need a cookie?

S. That's not fair. You didn't tell me about the papers before. This time I guess a paper clip is more important.

T. You're absolutely right. I didn't mention the papers at first, but when I did, you made a different choice. That's another thing that the mind's Comparer does. It pays attention to everything else about your situation before it helps you decide. We say that the Comparer is "context-sensitive."

S. Okay, I get it. The Comparer is pretty smart.

T. Yes, it's part of what makes you pretty smart. Your dog or a rabbit or a fish wouldn't understand about the paper clip. I think they'd all go for the cookie.

S. Fish don't eat cookies!

This is the first time that we introduce the idea of mind functioning in a context. Eventually, the idea of context connects to perception and awareness.

Conversation about thinking as a mind function

This next dialog begins the conversation about thinking and stresses that thinking establishes a person's individuality. Thinking means combining memory recall and projection with subtle and complicated use of mind-tools. The central role of attention is introduced.

T. Do you remember what minds do?

S. (distracted) Uh-huh.

T. So, tell me, what do minds do?

S. (sing-song) My mind is the part that makes me me.

T. Anything else?

S. (reciting) Remembers stuff … figures out what's going to happen … and compares cookies and paper clips.

T. That's good. Yes, your mind stores memories and recalls them. It creates something very much like a memory to help you imagine what could happen. And it helps you compare all sorts of things. There's another thing that your mind does that's important, in fact, the most important thing. Do you want to know about it?

S. (unenthusiastic) Uhhh … I guess … okay.

T. When you use your mind to remember things, imagine things, compare things, remember and project and compare more things and so on, and so on, it's called thinking. Thinking keeps going and going. It almost never stops. Your mind keeps doing what it does — just thinking — on and on, very fast.

S. (thoughtful) My Mom tells me things like that. Sometimes when she's mad, she says, "Oh! Why don't you just think before you do things!" Or, if I can't find my coat, she says, "Think! Where did you leave it?" This morning she said, "Think about what you want for your birthday." Is that what you mean?

T. Exactly. She wants you to use your mind to remember, imagine, plan, and compare. When you use it that way, you can solve all sorts of problems and figure out lots of things. That's why we have minds.

S. I thought I had a mind to make me me.

T. It does. Your mind and how you use it makes you you. Your Mom wants you to be the best you you can be, so she tells you to use your mind as well as you can. That's important because thinking is precisely what makes you who you are and how special you are.

S. You said that my mind is always busy. Does that mean I'm always thinking? I don't think I'm thinking.

T. Your mind is always busy, but it isn't always thinking. Sometimes a mind just sort of wanders around noticing things, remembering things, imagining things without any particular purpose. To get the thinking function going, we have to pay attention. Has anyone ever said to you, "Pay attention?"

S. (emphatic) That's what everybody says to me! "Pay attention to this. Pay attention to that." Parents and teachers all say that … a lot!

T. Can you figure out why they do that? Do they just want to make you mad?

S. Well, no. I guess they just want me to learn something or do something the way they want me to. Oh, I get it. They want me to use my mind's thinking function!

T. Absolutely. Thinking is how we learn, and thinking is how we control how we do most things.

S. So thinking is about school.

T. It's very important in school, but we can think and learn all the time: at school, at home, in the park, at the movies. Everywhere we are, we can think and learn things. The secret to learning is paying attention and turning on the thinking function of our minds. By the way, the part of your mind that controls the thinking is called the Reasoner.

S. (mischievously) Is there a reason for that?

T. You're teasing me, aren't you?

S. (triumphant smile) Yup.

Conversation about mind and choice

This next dialog with Bobby elaborates on the connection between what happens in the mind and what happens in reality. The dialog emphasizes the idea of rational choice.

S. (whining complaint) My parents never let me do anything. They're mean to me. They like my sister better. I'm thinking about running away from home.

T. You sound pretty unhappy. I can understand why you'd want things to change, but thinking about doing something and really doing it are very different. Understand?

S. Well, not really.

T. Yeah, I know this is hard. Let's take a few examples.

S. (gradually increasing interest) Okay, I guess.

T. Imagine your little sister broke your iPad. You're very mad. You want to hit her. You imagine hitting her, and then you imagine what your mother would say when she found out about it. What do you do? Do you hit your sister or not?

S. I don't hit her because I'd get in trouble … but I'm really mad.

T. That's right. Despite being super angry, you decided not to hit your sister. You used your mind to remember your iPad and remember your sister and remember your mother's feelings, and you decided not to hit. You made a good decision because you thought about it before you acted. We call that a rational decision.

S. I'm still mad.

T. Okay, could you use your mind to imagine something else you could do, like put your iPad on a high shelf where your sister can't reach?

S. (reluctantly) Yeah, I guess.

T. Here's another example. I asked you the other day, which was better a chocolate chip cookie or two oatmeal cookies. When I asked you, I didn't know what your answer would be. If you had gone home without ever answering my question, I still wouldn't know what you think. But you told me, so I knew that you thought two oatmeal cookies would be better than one chocolate chip. You used your mind to choose whether or not to tell me what you were thinking.

S. Now, I'm thinking about my iPad.

T. Other people only know about what you think when they see your choices, the things you say and the things you do. You chose not to hit your sister, and you chose to answer my question. I think

> you're a patient brother and a good kid. My thoughts about you are based only on what I've seen you do and say. If you considered hitting your sister, I have no way of knowing. It's all about the decisions and choices you make with your mind. But nobody else knows what you choose until you say something or do something. I bet your parents have told you, "Think before you act!" That's why.
>
> S. I'm gonna go see if my sister broke my iPad.

The 21st-Century Mind concepts help Bobby connect his thinking to his actions and the consequences of his actions to how the world perceives them. On the next page is a bit of children's rhyme* that could be learned by even the youngest. Ultimately the mind is connected to the child's self-image by simple things.

We can teach children, age four through elementary school, to think about the human mind as a gift and a profoundly useful set of tools and functions. Children should be able to answer questions like:

- What is a mind?
- What is a mental model?
- What are some of the things that a mind can do?

But, of course, education doesn't stop at elementary school. What follows in the next six shaded pages is an outline of how the topics of the 21st-Century Mind might be taught in middle and high schools. This is, of course, an enormous topic and will require substantial resources to actually implement. The outline is just a hint. Feel free to skip ahead.

21st-Century middle school topics

From late elementary school through middle school, exposure to the 21st-Century Mind deepens to include most of the model. Children change dramatically as they progress from babyhood to pre-adolescent, and teaching an expanded mental model is challenging. During these years, active games and group activities work most successfully. Songs, chants, and broad humor can help build a robust framework for the harder parts. Books — first readers through first chapter books ... will help teach the model.

---

* Much improved by Rebecca Lyles

To "If you're happy and you know it."

Oh, my mind is the part that makes me me.
Oh, my mind is the part that makes me me.
I can think, I can see
What a mind can really be

Oh, my mind is the part that makes me me.
Oh, my mind is the part that makes me me.
Not my brain or my heart,
They can make me very smart.
But my mind is the part that makes me me.

Oh, my mind is the part that makes me me.
Oh, my mind is the part that makes me me.
Not my hands or my feet,
They are really really neat.
But my mind is the part that makes me me.

Oh, your mind is the part that makes you you.
Oh, your mind is the part that makes you you.
What you think, what you know,
From your beanie to your toe,
Oh, your mind is the part that makes you you.

Oh, our minds are the parts that make us us.
Oh, our minds are the parts that make us us.
Better things you will find,
when you're sharing with your mind.
Oh, our minds are the parts that make us us.

Teaching and learning for these years will be a series of overlays, each containing more detail and depth than the previous layer.

Middle school review of elementary school topics

Each new topic will start with a quick and easy review of the fundamentals using the phrases and examples familiar to the preschool experience.

- What is a mind? "The part of me that makes me me!"
- What is a mental model? "A toy that I make with my imagination."
- What does a mind do? (Remember, Imagine, Think)

These basic concepts become more firmly rooted as they are repeated. The new material for the middle school age group will be introduced repeatedly as well, with each repetition adding breadth, depth, and detail.

The many uses of mental models in thinking

Mental models should be thoroughly explored. Mind-map tools should be introduced during middle school and are a powerful illustration of thought-bundles. When mental models are well understood, the mind's thinking tools can be added, and the complexity of thinking can begin to be investigated. Topics include:

- Simple identification and communication.
- Organization of hierarchies and abstractions.
- Comparison.
- Explanation.
- Planning.

Introduction to Perception

- Overview of the physical aspects and limitations of perception: seeing, hearing, touching, smelling, and tasting.
- Introduction of the distinction between attention and awareness and the critical role of attention.

Introduction to Beliefs, Values, Principles, and Rules

- We examine how beliefs influence decision-making. We need to get an appreciation of:
  - What it means to believe something

- How we get beliefs
- Examine the processes of investigation. Learn the nature of Principles and rules. Appreciate how principles and rules constrain choices and decisions. Topics:
  - Why we have rules.
  - Where rules come from. Principles or rules?
  - General rules and specific rules.
- Emphasizing that we learn many essential beliefs in school. Lessons provide the thought-bundles we need to think well and clearly.

Introducing the complex functions, strengths, and weaknesses of Memory

- We can remember either perceptions or thoughts.
- We usually remember only what we pay attention to.
- Memories are mental models and other thought-bundles with chronological and feeling data attached.

Middle School rubric for the 21ˢᵗ-Century Mind

When students leave middle school, they should understand the vocabulary of the 21ˢᵗ-Century Mind and appreciate the human mind's strengths and limitations.

- Understanding of mental models and how they are formed and manipulated by the mind's tools
- A proper grasp of the role and limitations of human senses and the difference between sensation and perception
- Clear understanding of the distinction between attention and awareness
- An appreciation for the hierarchy of the mindset and the ability to distinguish beliefs, principles, laws, rules, and expectations.
- A clear understanding of the central role of memory and an appreciation of the limitations of memory.

Middle schoolers should be ready to use the model's vocabulary and ideas to analyze the role of mental models in their day-to-day activities.

21ˢᵗ-Century high school topics

High School students expect increasing social, emotional, and academic independence. As they choose subjects to concentrate on, opportunities arise to apply the 21ˢᵗ-Century Mind as a framework for the concepts and details of all academic disciplines. Educators will decide where in the curriculum the ideas of the 21st-Century Mind model should be focused, but coordination will be required.

Young adults actively investigate human behavior, and they are often confronted with life-changing decisions. The 21st-Century Mind model is a suitable, neutral framework for discussion of these topics and can make dialog on complex or sensitive issues less emotionally loaded. In-class and independent study activities could include analyzing historical or literary characters (or popular fiction characters) in terms of the inclinations, mindsets, and mental models that drive or inhibit their behaviors. The language of the 21st-Century Mind model can facilitate role-playing.

A high school psychology course, if available, is a natural place to pursue the 21st-Century Mind model. Beyond psychology courses, it might be appropriate for advanced work on the nature of mind to be part of a science course exploring the relationship of mind and brain. Or the principal focus might be housed in the humanities, perhaps history, language arts, philosophy, or civics, where emphasis could be placed on the exploration of human interactions, relationships, and communications. Wherever the topics are raised, high school students should graduate with a full understanding of the 21st-Century Mind model. The next paragraphs provide a topic outline for high school.

Review elementary and middle school topics
- Basic terms: mind, mental model.
- Basic mind functions: remember, imagine, think.
- Uses of mental models in thinking: labels, organization, comparison, explanation, planning.
- Perception.
- Awareness and attention.

Additional topics about beliefs, principles, and rules
- Review of basics.
- What it means to believe something.
- How we get beliefs.
- How do we decide to believe something?

More about belief.

- How to tell if an assertion is a belief or something else.
- How beliefs relate to values.
- How beliefs and values are deeply embedded in our minds.
- How different people have different beliefs.
- How we feel when our beliefs conflict with someone else's.
- How we feel when some of our beliefs conflict with other things we believe.
- How popular ideas about beliefs and values are organized in the overall model of mind.

High school topics about principles and rules

Investigating the nature of principles and rules, including an appreciation of how principles and rules constrain choices and decisions. Topics:

- Principles and rules.
  - What they are.
  - Where they come from.
  - How they're different.
- Expectations and where they come from.
- How principles and expectations relate to beliefs.
- What happens when there are internal conflicts.

Conceptual balances as an essential part of diversity

People have different inclinations. We are just naturally different in a vast number of ways that appear to be built-in. Some of these can be important in how we make decisions.

Here are some to consider:

- Risk-taking/ avoiding
- Introvert/extrovert
- Leader/ follower
- Abstracter/concretizer
- Spiritual/material
- Sustainer/transformer

These conceptual balances might change as we have new experiences, but they are likely to change slowly.

Variation in inclinations is a positive for the species as a whole but may not suit a specific individual or even a small group in a particular context.

High school on mind-tools and the "rational mind"

Thinking is the most complicated function of the mind. When we think we use a set of mental tools.

Rememberer and **Projector** both suggest versions of mental models, and both are selective and influenced by beliefs, principles, and expectations.

Comparer is the mind's judge.
- The same or not, and, if different, how different.
- Similar and how similar.
- Satisfactory or not.

The **Conceptualizer** makes and modifies mental models.
- Abstracts and generalizes mental models, cause-and-effect relationships, and other thought-bundles.
- Creates connections and relationships among mental models, thought-bundles, and feelings.

The **Feeler** has deep connections with the subconscious and physical brain. It:
- Labels mental models with emotions.
- Reads them back.

The **Reasoner** operates with other tools to generate the sensation of understanding.
- Reasoning to a conclusion is thinking.
- Reasoning to a specific target is proving.
- Reasoning that remains unresolved is worrying.

High school material about memory
- Review of basics: We can remember either perceptions or thoughts; we usually remember only what we pay attention to; the memories are thought-bundles with chronology and feelings attached.

- At best, memories have no more correct information than the perceptions and thinking that formed them.
- Repetitive recall can strengthen memories, but it also shapes and alters them.
- Each recall occurs in a unique context that shapes the thought-bundles in use and affects how the recalled thought-bundles are stored.

What filters do and where they come from

- Filters are the mind's mechanism for applying inclination and the mindset (belief, principles, and rules). Both formation and recall of memories are affected by filters.
- Recalling memories makes them more durable but may change them in the process.
- Projection and expectation use the same processes as recollection, but for a different purpose.
- Filters expedite decision-making and intention-formation.
- Biases are filters that distort perceptions, memories, or other thinking in a consistent direction.

The nature of conscious and subconscious

- We talk about conscious mind and subconscious mind, but there is just one mind — complex, unified, and integrated.
- The experience of having a mind changes along a spectrum of attention.
- The spectrum of consciousness is universal but varies in range, intensity, and volatility among individuals.
- "Up-spectrum" the mind is concerned with doing.
- "Down-spectrum" the mind is concerned with being and feeling.
- Memory formation works best up-spectrum and poorly down-spectrum.
- Outer consciousness dominates up-spectrum, and inner consciousness dominates down-spectrum.
- Up-spectrum we act in the here and now, Down-spectrum we move into the realm of memory. There is a bright line, but we cross it again and again, often without noticing.
- There is more information flow from consciousness into memory when alert and more flow from memory into consciousness when less alert.

Investigation topics and challenges for high school

From the very earliest introduction of the 21st-Century Mind model, there are opportunities to ask questions that a student or a group of students can investigate. It is not necessary or even desirable that such investigations produce the "right" answer. The following are some the many possible topics and challenges.

- Who has a mind — babies, animals, plants, rocks, computers? How can you tell?
- Andrew and Jennifer are fraternal twins; Bill and Bob are identical twins. How many minds do these four people have?
- Draw a line through any of these which is not a human sense: hearing, playing, seeing, smelling, tasting, thinking, touching, writing.
- Choose one of the five primary human senses and investigate the limitations of the sense.
- Name the parts of the human mind and explain (in one sentence each) what the component does.
- Give an example of a mental model of something that is not real. Give an example of a mental model of something real but invisible.
- Pick a historical figure from your studies and describe where you think that person would fall on the conceptual balance scales. Give your opinion on which conceptual balance(s) was (were) most important in this person's role in history.
- Identify which of these statements (from a list) might be principles. Label each statement useful-principle, harmful-principle, not a principle. (extra credit: if it's not a principle, what is it?).

Conversation about "Why do I have to study that?"

Teachers hear the question; students asked it (if only silently) — "Why do I have to study that? I'll never use it!" The question arises early with things like multiplication tables. It is asked again and again about material as varied as the periodic table, geography, fractions, names of the planets, dissecting a worm, and the works of Shakespeare.

Students deserve better than, "It's in the curriculum" or "it's on the test." When a youngster acquires a suitable mental model of the mind, the answer becomes more natural.

Here is a conversation between our tutor and, Sam, an adolescent who has been exposed to the 21st-Century Mind model since preschool. Sam has rebelled against studying algebra, science, and social studies. He wants to be a musician … or maybe an actor.

T. Hey, Sam, I hear you want to quit going to school.

S. Yeah, well, that stuff is a waste of time. Math and that other stuff has nothing to do with me.

T. (sympathetic) I hear you, it's a lot of work, so why do it, right?

S. Right. I guess. I don't mind working, but I just don't get why I should study stuff that I'll never use or care about.

T. (nodding sympathetically) Sam, do you know anything about boxing?

S. I've seen it on TV. I watch it sometimes with my Dad.

T. Maybe you've seen some scenes of training — pounding heavy bags, hitting the speed bag, maybe jumping rope, or doing push-ups?

S. Yeah, I've seen that, mostly in movies. Dad likes the old Rocky movies.

T. Good. Now let's do a thought experiment. Imagine a mental model of a boxing ring — ropes, crowd, bell, etc. Got it? Now use your Projector to imagine a boxing match — two guys, hands up, getting ready to punch each other. Now (this is the hard part) imagine one of the guys drops to the mat and starts doing push-ups.

S. (surprised) You're kidding right. That's stupid!

T. Okay, let say instead that he pulls a rope out of his trunks and starts jumping. Does this make sense?

S. (emphatic) Of course not.

T. What if he turns his back and starts hitting an imaginary speed bag or starts pounding on the ring post like it was a heavy bag?

S. That's stupid too.

T. I agree, but here's the question: why do boxers do all of those things when they're training, even though they never do them in an actual fight?

S. (thoughtful) Ohhh … I get it. The boxer does those things to train for the fight, to get in shape. So, I guess you're trying to tell me school is like training for something.

T. Well, yes. School is like training for your life. The boxer's life isn't about skipping rope, and he's not looking for a job as a bag pounder or a floor pusher. He does those things to get ready. You have things to do to get prepared too.

S. But I'm not getting ready to be a scientist; I'm gonna make music or go on the stage. Why should I train doing math homework?

T. That's a good question. Some of the subjects that we ask you to learn in school seem pointed at specific jobs, but the big picture is that we are helping you equip yourself with a wide range of mental models, cause-and-effect relationships, and fact-bundles for two reasons.

    First, even though neither of us knows exactly what part of the stuff you learn in school will be useful, a lot will be. We teachers plan it that way.

    Second, learning to think and learning to learn are critical skills you need no matter what direction you take in your life. So, if you don't like algebra, just think of it as one of the gym workouts you need to prepare for the main event — your life.

We would like it if every graduate could articulate an answer to the "why should I study this" question. Clarity about the value and workings of the human mind can take us closer to that positive place. What a wonder it would be to hear each student voice thoughts like these:

- Knowledge is the total of all the things we know — beliefs, cause-and-effect models, memories, and the entire complex of thought-bundles and their connections.
- Studying puts more mental models and thought-bundles into my mind, increasing my knowledge.
- The mental models and other thought-bundles we acquire in school have been chosen to help us organize and understand all the knowledge we acquire.
- This collection of mental models and thought-bundles (and the practice we get using them) is called an education.

- Education is offered by my teachers but earned by my efforts.
- More knowledge is almost always more valuable than less knowledge. A clear idea of the extent and boundaries of our knowledge is a sign of wisdom.

Clarity about the value of general knowledge leads naturally to understanding the importance of a broad liberal education. The following paragraphs employ the vocabulary of the 21st-Century Mind model to answer the "why should I study ..." question for the major education disciplines as they have been understood since the Enlightenment.

Why should I study math?

Most early experience with math is simple arithmetic taught mostly as memorization. It's mostly boring, but no matter how clever we are, we can't run before we can walk. Certain fact-bundles like addition and multiplication tables are necessary before we get to the most useful parts of math. Besides, everybody must get through learning the basic rules of arithmetic, simple algebra, and at least little slices of geometry and trigonometry to understand modern life. A modern human without basic math is a cripple.

- Without the basic mathematical mental models — for example, counting, sorting into equal numbers and amounts, simplest sums and differences — we are barely human. Something so fundamental to humanity must be the foundation of something important.
- Mathematics gives us mental models of things we observe but not understand (For example, the motions of the sun and planets). Mathematics is a power-tool for the Projector part of minds.
- If you want to understand the world and be successful in it, some mathematics is essential; more mathematics is better.
- Math provides rigorous mental models for the Comparer mind-tool and makes it more useful.
- Biases are much more difficult to attach to mathematical results than to rhetorical assertions. Thinking by the rules of mathematics is more likely to be correct than guesses and opinions.
- It's no accident that human society and technology development — starting slowly in prehistory and accelerating exponential-

ly through the Ancients, the Enlightenment, to the modern age — has paralleled the creation and spread of mathematical mental models.

- Mathematics provides the most important mental models ever developed by humans for advancing our security, welfare, and comfort. Science and technology are impossible without math.

Why should I study science?

- Science is the best way we have to discover genuine cause-and-effect relationships.
- Science is about why and how the world is as it is.
- Science provides trusted mental models for investigation (How did it get this way? or What would be different if …?) and for forecasting (What happens if …?).
- Science provides mental models that explain physical events. How else might we answer questions like: why does iron rust and gold doesn't? why do balls bounce and birds don't? or why does the moon have phases and the sun does not?
- We trust scientific mental models because science uses procedures, guidelines, and safeguards to reduce the biases, shortcomings, and vagaries of the human mind.
- Guesses and opinions about reality do not serve us as reliably as scientific mental models established by research and experimentation.

Why should I study humanities?

Science gives us the mental models to investigate, understand, and project changes in the physical world. Humanities give us the mental models to investigate, understand, and project human behavior in our social world. Humanities are fields of study where we learn different mental models for different purposes.

- ***First language.*** We study our own language because the better we know it, the better we communicate thought-bundles to other people who also know it. Communicating about mental models is the fundamental process by which our human species enhances our ability to survive. Better communication improves coordination, cooperation with other people, and conflict resolution.

- **Modern languages.** We study modern foreign languages so that we can communicate mental models and our thoughts about them to people who know those other languages. Enhancing the circle of people with whom we can communicate is a contribution to our individual welfare and to our group's ability to coordinate, cooperate, and, if necessary, to compete.

- **Classical languages.** We study ancient languages because the study provides general mental models and abstract categories for describing and analyzing language. The mental models of things, events, and feelings embedded in ancient languages can also give clues to the mindsets and mental models of ancient people.

- **History.** We study history to improve our thinking about human behavior. History compiles observations of how humans have behaved. Historians weave the facts of the past into mental models of human behavior, which can be applied to explain why human affairs are the way they are or to forecast how human affairs may change.

- **Archeology.** Archeology is history by different methods. Through a study of human development and material culture, archeology applies the rigor of science to the study of past human behavior. Archeology attempts to uncover early mental models of how primitive humans understood reality and how essential learning grew over time.

- **Philosophy.** Philosophy and comparative religion strengthen the mind's ability to answer — or at least investigate — difficult questions. Philosophy provides mental models of abstract thinking and labels for arguments and fallacies. Philosophy describes how past thinkers examined questions about knowledge, ethical behavior, and the nature of reality and beauty. It addresses questions of belief and values. Philosophy helps us understand the role of principles, laws, rules, and expectations as boundaries between actions we might consider and what is "unthinkable."

- **Art.** We study art and music to learn the various crafts' mental models and understand the connections between art and how the mind associates perceptions with feelings.

❧ ❧ ❧ ❧ ❧ ❧

This chapter has outlined a course of study illustrating a possible pedagogic progression. We assert that we're all better off when we teach this stuff to our kids, and they don't have to wait for college (or beyond) to begin learning it. Not everyone agrees. The next chapter examines and answers some critical arguments.

Based on image by Micaela Parente

Chapter 16
Critical Arguments

EVERY IDEA WORTH discussing has supporters and critics. The following are some of the criticisms leveled at the contents of this book … and the answers.

Criticism … there is no scientific basis for this description of how a mind works.

Answer. While the description of the 21st-Century Mind model is grounded in two sources of knowledge – science and personal subjective experience … this book does not present itself as science, more like engineering. It stands on its potential usefulness.

The model encompasses scientific knowledge from psychology, cognitive science, and all the associated research into the functioning of a brain and its relationship to a mind. "Encompass" in the sense that the model is not inconsistent with what we know about brains and bodies and the minds that inhabit them. Our knowledge of brain function advances quickly. If contradictions arise, the model should evolve only enough to avoid falsehood while maintaining the necessary simplicity and level of abstraction. We can never teach our children everything, but we should never teach them falsehoods.

Criticism ... there is no mathematical basis.

Answer. There is indeed no mathematical basis for either the model or the assertion that absorbing this model can lead to better thinking. This criticism, however, is a *non sequitur*. How would mathematics be useful to the child or adult who knows little or none?

Mathematical models of mind do exist. For example, *The Structure of Intelligence: A New Mathematical Model of Mind* (Goertzel 1993), but it contains advanced mathematics from at least four different specialties plus quantum mechanics... more mathematics than any non-expert is likely to follow. Hardly "suitable" for teaching children or young adults about their superpower.

Criticism ... brain research makes this unnecessary.

Critics argue that bottom-up understanding will make the idea of mind irrelevant. Eventually, they say, we will know everything we need to know to explain the functions of the mind in terms of the workings of the brain.

Answer. Scientific reductionism tells us that biology is explained by chemistry; chemistry is explained by physics; and physics explains everything. The objection stated here is that biology will explain the mind, and hence, we will understand it all: an ambitious claim and a very long way from being proven correct. Much modern thinking about consciousness rejects this reductionism.

Most important, the criticism misses the point. This book is about minds, not brains. How would exhaustive knowledge of brains make me a better decision-maker? If I know and understand the physical and chemical details of engines, tires, and brakes, do I know how to drive? If I know the intimate details of how Stradivarius built violins, am I a violinist? Of course not. The purpose of the 21st-Century Mind model is to provide an easily understood way to discuss the workings of the human mind and make it easier to teach how to use it better.

Criticism ... the concept of thinking, as presented, obscures all the hard parts of explaining the mind.

Critics disparage the model's small number of tools that perform elementary mental operations – Rememberer, Projector, Comparer,

Reasoner, Feeler, and Conceptualizer. They argue that these abstractions sweep the complexity of the mind's activity under the rug labeled "thinking." It doesn't explain how to think.

Answer. The overarching business of education is to teach how to think. Education provides the facts, process descriptions, and examples from which the mental models of reality are drawn. The point of this book and the 21st-Century Mind model is not to replace education, but to make it better by providing a framework on which the justification, details, and processes of education can hang.

Listing the elementary tools of mind is a bit like enumerating the contents of a good workshop or a good kitchen. A good woodworker and a good baker are alike in needing to understand the tools they use. A good thinker should also understand the tools of the craft. Of course, that's not enough. A woodworker needs wood, and a baker needs flour; a thinker needs mental models of reality.

Further, the woodworker needs a design, and the baker needs a recipe, but neither craftsman produces a good result without experience. So, too, the thinker needs to practice the craft. When the thinker has the mental models and has practiced with them, we say he's learned something. Enough models and sufficient practice, we say he's educated.

Criticism … people already know all this.

Critics argue there is nothing new in this book, that any good course in psychology has all this information and more.

Answer. Yes, some people know all this, but too few. And, some don't know any of this; too many. Good thinking about thinking shouldn't be rare, optional, or privileged.

Except among experts and specialists, there are no coherent mental models of mind, and among those experts and specialists, there is little broad agreement on a simple set of terms and concepts. The point of the book is that, if we all knew about the functioning of the mind and discussed how we use it, we would be likely to make better decisions with fewer errors. However, so far, there is no suitable mental model that can underlie all our other teaching and learning.

Criticism … too abstract for school children.

Some say that the ideas of mind, mental model, tools for thinking, etc. are abstract and too complicated for school children to grasp. They argue, "Even adults don't understand this stuff. Spending time and money in schools on topics like this would be a waste."

Answer. Children learn abstract concepts from repeated exposure to examples that provide mental hooks and patterns. Even youngsters as young as four grasp the meaning of abstract words like "happy" and "sad." None of the concepts in the 21st-Century Mind model are more complicated than most elementary school topics in arithmetic, science, social studies, language arts, music, art, or reading.

Criticism … teachers already have too much to do.

Some complain, "Teachers are already overburdened with the required material and find it difficult to cover even basics. It is unreasonable to load on even more."

Answer. Once the idea of the 21st-Century Mind model takes hold in the teaching community, its usefulness becomes evident, and it is a net benefit to teachers. The common terminology of the model will help explain the motivation and content of all the subjects that comprise an education. Many of the disagreements among teachers, parents, and students can be avoided by finding clarity about what, why, and how teaching leads to learning and learning leads to a more successful life.

Criticism … too much emphasis on avoiding thinking errors would undermine confidence.

A thoughtful critic might say, once this model of mind is internalized, an unavoidable consequence is learning about how many ways the mind contributes to making mistakes. If we teach children to mistrust their minds, they might become lost in fear, uncertainty, and paralysis.

Answer. This is a serious concern. Too much emphasis on the limitations of the mind could undermine an individual's confidence. Education must balance its focus on limitations with a strong emphasis on the unique strengths we, as humans, possess because we have minds. Instruction on how humans, as a species, have progressed beyond the bounds of instinct because of our consciousness may be required. Teaching the unique strengths of all humans and the truly magnificent gift of human minds may well open new avenues for discussing our historical errors of racism and ethnocentrism.

We have reached the end of our discussion of the 21st-Century Mind model —its parts, its functions, its benefits – and our observations about teaching it. The next and final chapter outlines a plan for taking the 21st-Century Mind from slogan to success.

Based on image by Diego PH

Chapter 17
Make It Happen

You're convinced ... *a suitable mental model of mind leads to better thinking.* You share the goal of introducing the 21ˢᵗ-Century Mind model into the national education system. Excellent; how do we make that happen? Here are the steps:

- **Vision.** State clearly where we want to go and what we want to accomplish. Describe the desired future state.
- **Pursuits.** Consider and document a small number of essential pursuits to bring about the desired future state.
- **Measurements.** Establish measurements of the desired future state and the pursuits so that we can monitor progress.

And here's how we start — with a vision. "If you don't know where you're going, a map won't help."

Vision statement: define the desired future state

Ask these questions: What will it be like when we're done? How will we know if we are making progress? How will we know if we have succeeded? The answers describe the desired future state. Here's a start.

When this project has succeeded:

- Children and adults will discuss thinking with a common vocabulary and understanding of the mind's functions.
- Adults will know the significant sources of decision-making error and the human mind's limitations. Children will learn these in school.
- The quality of decision-making will have improved.

The first two points require input measurement. The third point, more difficult to quantify, requires measures of the results.

Top level pursuits: tasks to bring about the desired future state

Accomplish these seven top-level pursuits:

- **Leadership pursuit.** Organize a leader-group and procedures to guide and fund the project.
- **Collateral pursuit.** Prepare and produce 21ˢᵗ-Century Mind collateral materials.
- **Influencers pursuit.** Publicize the 21ˢᵗ-Century Mind to influencers.
- **Teachers pursuit.** Introduce the 21ˢᵗ-Century Mind model to the education establishment.
- **Parents pursuit.** Introduce the 21ˢᵗ-Century Mind model to the general population, especially parents.
- **Curriculum pursuit.** Introduce the 21ˢᵗ-Century Mind model into the general curriculum and implement success measures.
- **Evergreen pursuit.** Periodically review and revise the vision statement and the top-level pursuits

These seven essential pursuits are described in more detail in the following sections.

Leadership Group and 21ˢᵗ-Century Mind Foundation

First, a small group of people will be assembled to find the necessary start-up resources and to do the start-up work. This small, informal group will expand as the movement grows. Eventually, the leadership-group will be formalized. In time the leadership group will mature, and the work will become more demanding.

- Establish the 21ˢᵗ-Century Mind Foundation formal structure with appropriate legal and accounting processes. Engage advisors to promote the model and actively seek adoption into the American education system.

- Begin, under the direction of the leadership group, to establish and monitor key performance measurements for individual pursuits and the movement overall.

Prepare and produce collateral

- This book is a start, but a great deal of promotional, educational, and training material will be required throughout the life of the project.
- Website(s), blog(s), brochures, manuals, podcasts, videos, learning games, children's books, etc.
- Test materials

Gather influencers and supporters

- Figure out who the influencers are: educators, developmental psychologists, interested politicians, philanthropists, and activists.
- Recruit a critical mass of influencers to participate and support the project.
- Identify and recruit people with the necessary skills — writers, teachers, speakers, fundraisers, etc.
- Prepare for significant push-back to the 21st-Century Mind proposals.

Major decision point

At some time, fairly early in the development of the 21st-Century Foundation, the Foundation leadership should take a careful look at whether the objectives of the Foundation are best served by undertaking the national roll-out of the model alone or with a more mature and well-established organization.

Establish a presence with the education establishment

- Expose educators to the ideas and explain the benefits. Emphasize the minimal impact of classroom time and savings from sharing vocabulary and concepts across disciplines.
- Identify and run trials. Measure the costs and impacts on classroom time. Publicize the trials.
- Seek endorsements from the education establishment – professional groups, lobbying groups, unions, etc.

- Introduce the ideas and benefits. Set up separate "education" efforts for public school organizations, private school organizations, and home-school organizations.
- Establish working relationships with the textbook and on-line learning industries.

Establish a presence with the general public

- Make the general population, especially parents, aware of the 21st-Century Mind as essential to every child's better life prospects.
- A massive promotion and public relations effort will be required.
- "Fewer mistakes, fewer bad decisions, fewer poor choices make a better, healthier, safer life. We owe it to our kids."

Introduce the 21st-Century Mind model into the general curriculum and monitor success

- Use the 21st-Century Mind Foundation to promote the model into the education curriculum for school systems throughout the country.
- Lobby state boards of education and individual school districts and seek an addition to the State's and school districts' education standards.
- Monitor success by tracking numbers of schools, teachers, and students who have adopted a 21st-Century Mind learning module.
- Use polls to monitor the model's acceptance.

Periodically review and revise the vision statement and the top level pursuits

- Require, as a fundamental principle, that each pursuit should build into its task cycles a periodic review of goals, structure, and measures.
- Review and revise the overall vision of the 21st-Century Mind foundation on a regular cycle.

❧ ❧ ❧ ❧ ❧ ❧ ❧

This chapter has outlined the work required to introduce a suitable model of mind into our schools. Join in and follow our progress toward teaching children about their superpower at the 21st-Century Mind Foundation website. Visit

www.21stCenturyMind.org.

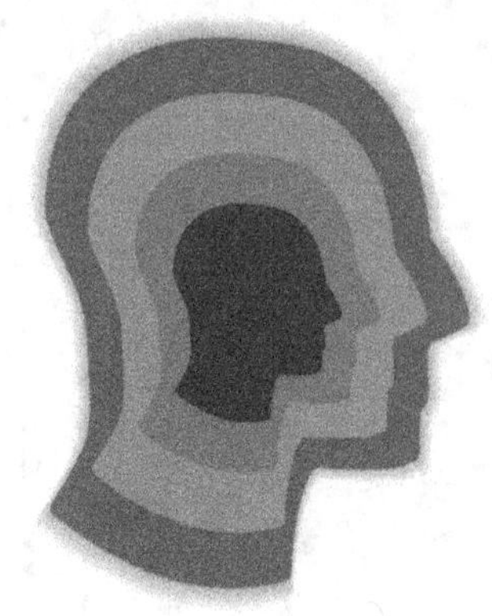

Glossary

Analysis	The application of knowledge by the mind's tools to narrowing down alternatives to "realistic" possibilities when making decisions.
Attention	A mind function which focuses on a particular facet of awareness.
Awareness	A combination of brain-function and mind-function by which perceptions like vision or hearing are matched against memory and attached to thoughts or made into whole new thoughts.
Belief engine	Developmental Biologist Lewis Wolpert's phrase to label the peculiarly human need to understand cause-and-effect and the workings of our reality.
Conceptual balance	An abstract, but real, general characteristic or inclination of a person's mind such as likes, dislikes, and attitudes.
Confirmation bias	A mental filter applied to some part of the mind's information flow that confirms an existing belief.
Consciousness	What we experience as our attention shifts from moment to moment.
Core values	Those things people generally agree are valuable.
Decision-making	The process of forming an intention.
Decisions	The choices we make and actions we take.

Dualism	The understanding by philosophers that mind and body are different things.
Education	The process of accumulating beliefs or the result of the accumulation. Receiving new information, storing it in memory, and recalling it when useful.
Event model	Any memory information thought-bundle that describes a change
Expectation	Mental model of a future state produced by the Projector.
Feeler	The mind/brain tool that connects emotional states in the mind with specific physical or neurological states in the body and vice versa.
Filter	Any influencer that modifies a mind's information flow into, out of, or within the mind by tweaking, twisting, transforming, or obscuring the information that constitutes our observed reality. Biases are exerted through filters.
Forecast	A mental model of a future state produced by the Projector.
Free will.	The human gift and burden of being able to balance the efficiency of subconscious decision-making with the ability to examine the filtered version of reality and test it consciously. The ability to think before we act.
Hard Problem (of consciousness)	Explaining how the personal experience of mind and body are connected,
I (me)	The individual mind's lived experience.

Idea	Any memory information thought-bundle.
Inclinations	See conceptual balance
Information cluster	Any memory information thought-bundle made up of other information thought-bundles.
Intelligence	The fundamental capability by which humans combine experience and knowledge to solve a problem, determine a course of action, or understand a complicated situation.
Intention, Intention formation	A function of the mind that seeks to bring about a future state: the intention precedes invoking the effector system, which brings about change in the physical world.
Judgment	Consideration of all that we could do with a narrow focus on what we are willing to do. This narrowed focus involves applying principles
Knowledge	The aggregate of all our mental models, memories, and thought-bundles obtained from personal experience and from others.
Learning	Knowledge. The process by which we adjust our information bundles through direct-experience, studying, and trusting information we get from others

Meme (mental model or thought)	A memory information thought-bundle for carrying a cultural idea, symbol, or practice that can be transmitted from one mind to another through writing, speech, gestures, or rituals.
Memory	The part of the mind/brain where, when I'm not thinking about something I've learned or noticed, the associated information bundles are stored.
Mental image	A memory information thought-bundle connected to a visual depiction
Mental model	Any memory information bundle which represents a thing, a process, or a cause-and-effect relationship.
Mind-tools	The 21st-Century model of mind includes six abstract mind-tools that, when combined, carry out the process of thinking. Specifically: Rememberer, Projector, Comparer, Reasoner, Conceptualizer, and Feeler
Mindset	The collection of mental models and constraints that provide boundaries separating our willing choices from all the other possibilities. A mindset includes beliefs, values, principles, and rules.
My Mind	The part of me that makes me "me."
Pathways (per Gelernter)	Series of connected thoughts learned (or constructed by the Conceptualizer) employed by the conscious mind.
Personality traits	Another term for conceptual balances, inclinations, subconscious preferences, proclivities, or drives.

Principle	A useful statement of how the mind constrains intention formation in a particular situation
Process schema	Any memory information thought-bundle that describes a series of event models
Projector	The mind-tool that uses fact-bundles and cause-and-effect relations from memory to figure out how events connect. Answers questions: Why did this happen? How did this happen? How did things get this way? What happens if …?
Proving	The process in which the Reasoner starts with a specific projected mental model objective and applies the other tools of the mind one after another to figure out what additional mental models and what path would be required to produce the goal.
Qualia	The features of an information thought-bundle that represent the ways things seem to us – color, shape, size, etc.
Reasoner	The mind-tool that applies the other tools of the mind one after another to create a sense of understanding.
Reasoning	Conscious mind activity directed to a conscious goal.
Referent	Any memory information thought-bundle to which a specific label has been connected.
Rememberer	The part of our minds that brings memories to our attention.

Thought-bundle	Collection of information, loosely binding a variety of information (including other thought-bundles) and containing associations and links to other thought-bundles.
Values	The things we believe are important.
Vices	Actions that tend to diminish the likelihood of satisfying our needs.
Virtues	Actions that tend to improve the likelihood that we will satisfy our needs.
Worrying	The process in which the Reasoner applies the mind's other tools one after another but fails to conclude.

References

Alcock, James E., *Belief: What it means to believe and why our convictions are so compelling*. Amherst, New York: Prometheus Books, 2018. Print.

BBC NEWS, *Statistics reveal Britain's 'Mr and Mrs Average,'* October 13, 2010, www.bbc.com/news/uk-11534042

Bransford, John. *How people learn: brain, mind, experience, and school*. Washington, D.C.: National Academy Press, 2000. Print.

Brown, Donald E. Human universals. Philadelphia: Temple University Press, 1991. Print.

Chabad.Org, *The 613 Commandments (Mitzvot)*, accessed January 2020, Mendy Hecht, Chabad-Lubavitch Media Center, www.chabad.org/library/article_cdo/aid/756399/jewish/The-613-Commandments-Mitzvot.htm

Chabris, Christopher, Simons, Daniel, *The Invisible Gorilla*, accessed 1-31-2020, http://www.theinvisiblegorilla.com/gorilla_experiment.html

Chalmers, David J., Scientific American, *The Puzzle of Conscious Experience*, December 1995, Vol. 273, No. 6, pp. 80-86

Dragoi, Valentin, Neuroscience Online, *Chapter 14: Visual Processing: Eye and Retina*, accessed 1-31-2020, McGovern Medical School at UTHealth, nba.uth.tmc.edu/neuroscience/m/s2/chapter14.html

Dragoi, Valentin, Neuroscience Online, *Chapter 15: Cortical Pathways*, accessed 1-31-2020, McGovern Medical School at UTHealth, nba.uth.tmc.edu/neuroscience/m/s2/chapter15.html

Dweck, Carol S. Mindset: the new psychology of success. New York: Random House, 2006. Print.

Gelernter, David H. *The Tides of Mind: uncovering the spectrum of consciousness*. New York: Liveright Publishing Corporation, a division of W.W. Norton & Company, Independent Publishers, 2016. Print.

Goertzel, Ben, *The Structure of Intelligence: A New Mathematical Model of Mind*, Heidelberg, Springer-Verlag, 1993.

Grossman, Samantha, TIME, *Here's a Picture of the World's Tallest Man and the World's Shortest Man Shaking Hands*, November 13, 2014, time.com/3583663/worlds-tallest-man-shortest-man-shaking-hands/

Henrichon, Susan J., Sciencing, *Examples of Sensory Adaptation*, April 24, 2017, Leaf Group Ltd., sciencing.com/examples-sensory-adaptation-14224.html

How People Learn: Brain, Mind, Experience, and School: Expanded Edition (2000), *Chapter: 4 How Children Learn*, www.nap.edu/read/9853/chapter/7

Maslow, A.H., *A theory of human motivation. Psychological Review. (1943)., 50 (4): 370–96.* CiteSeerX 10.1.1.334.7586. doi:10.1037/h0054346 – *via psychclassics.yorku.ca.*

Minsky, Marvin. The society of mind. New York: Simon and Schuster, 1986. Print.

Mischel, Walter, *Ebbesen, Ebbe B., "Attention In Delay Of Gratification."* Journal of Personality and Social Psychology, *(1970), 16 (2): 329–337.* doi:10.1037/h0029815. ISSN 0022-3514.

OLogy, *Optical Illusions and How They Work*, accessed 1-31-2020, American Museum of Natural History, www.amnh.org/explore/ology/brain/optical-illusions-and-how-they-work

Park, N., Peterson, C., & Seligman, M.E.P. (2004). *Strengths of character and well-being. Journal of Social and Clinical Psychology,* 23, 603–619.

Price-Mitchell, Marilyn, Psychology Today, *What Is Education? Insights from the World's Greatest Minds*, May 12, 2014, Sussex Publishers, LLC., www.psychologytoday.com/us/blog/the-moment-youth/201405/what-is-education-insights-the-worlds-greatest-minds

Rosenblum, Lawrence D., *The McGurk Effect*, accessed 1-31-2020, faculty.ucr.edu/~rosenblu/VSMcGurk.html

ScienceDaily, *ScienceDaily*, June 7, 2018, www.sciencedaily.com/releases/2018/06/180607135206.htm.

Society of Professional Journalists, *SPJ Code of Ethics*, Revised September 6, 2014 at 4:49 p.m., CT at SPJ's National Convention in Nashville, Tenn, www.spj.org/ethicscode.asp

Tononi, Giulio and Koch, Christof, Philosophical Transactions B, *Review article Consciousness: here, there and everywhere?* May 19, 2015, doi.org/10.1098/rstb.2014.0167

Tononi, Giulio., Phi: a voyage from the brain to the soul. New York: Pantheon, 2012.

Trafton, Anne, MIT News, *How expectation influences perception*, July 15, 2019, Massachusetts Institute of Technology, news.mit.edu/2019/how-expectation-influences-perception-0715

Wieber, Frank, Thürmer, J. Lukas, and Gollwitzer, Peter M., *Promoting the translation of intentions into action by implementation intentions: behavioral effects and physiological correlates,* Front Hum Neurosci. 2015; 9: 395, 2015 July 14.

Wired, *Here's scientific proof your brain was designed to be distracted,* August 22, 2018, Condé Nast Britain, www.wired.co.uk/article/brain-distraction-procrastination-science.

Acknowledgments

Books start full of errors as do minds. Experience and care gradually make them better. A cadre of helpful thinkers has provided invaluable experience as this book has grown and matured. Without my "friendly readers" — teachers, psychologists, scholars, friends, and family – this book would not exist. Many thanks to you all and special thanks to those of you who have been most critical ... er, I mean, constructive with your comments and corrections.

I wish to call out specifically: Professor Gordon Sollars who put the book in historical context; Rebecca Lyles of TextCPR who greatly improved the dialogs and tone; Betty Pachciarz who hunted down dozens of comma-splices; Helga Minderjahn who made essential contributions to the graphics and images; Jill Hungsburg who sharpened the book's focus; Professor David Gelernter who kindly allowed me to paraphrase his work on consciousness; Dr. Gary James who recruited early readers, and, of course Rosi Hasenyager who put up with the author's ups and downs and offered him care and support while the book had its growing pains.

Image by Crawford Jolly

Index

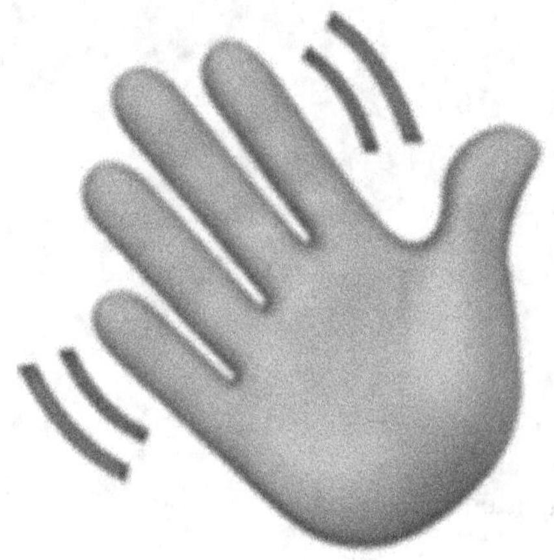

Join!

The 21st-Century Mind Foundation is the organization dedicated to this simple logic:

- Human beings need to think better — more clearly and more consciously.
- We should start by teaching our kids about their minds – their human superpower.
- The need for better thinking is more important now than it's ever been. We can't teach about thinking if we can't talk about minds.

Be clear; we are talking about minds, not brains. A suitable mental model of the human mind is essential to any meaningful discussion about thinking.

The purpose of the 21st Century Mind Foundation is to bring about our vision. We work to:

- Give children and adults a common vocabulary and understanding of the mind's functions so that they can discuss thinking.
- Make sure adults know the major sources of decision-making error and the human mind's limitations and that children learn these in school.
- Measurably improve the quality of American decision-making.

The Foundation addresses these major tasks:

- Organize a leader-group to guide and fund the Foundation
- Prepare and produce 21st Century Mind collateral materials.
- Publicize the 21st Century Mind to influencers, teachers, parents and the general population.
- Introduce the 21st Century Mind model into the general curriculum.

Sign up. History beckons!